This

The
Little Book of
PIES

The
Little Book of
PIES

Sweet and Savoury Pies and Tarts
for All Year Round

MARIKA GAUCI

Published by Square Peg 2014

2 4 6 8 10 9 7 5 3 1

Copyright © Marika Gauci

Text © Marika Gauci

Marika Gauci has asserted her rights under the Copyright, Designs and Patents Act 1988 to be identified as the author of this work

The Random House Group Limited Reg. No. 954009

Addresses for companies within The Random House Group Limited can be found at:
www.randomhouse.co.uk

A CIP catalogue record for this book is available from the British Library

ISBN 9780224095754

The Random House Group Limited supports the Forest Stewardship Council®(FSC®), the leading international forest-certification organisation. Our books carrying the FSC label are printed on FSC®-certified paper. FSC is the only forest-certification scheme supported by the leading environmental organisations, including Greenpeace. Our paper procurement policy can be found at www.randomhouse.co.uk/environment

Design: ClarkevanMeurs Design
Photography: Sarah Cuttle
Author photo: Susanne Aichele
Copy editor: Laura Herring
Proofreader: Annie Lee

Printed and bound in China by C&C Offset Printing Co., Ltd

Dedicated to Clive, our daughter Phaedra
and my mother Maureen

Contents

❿ SWEET RECIPES 82

Living the PIE Life

I run a cookery school and, since 2009, I have been giving the only British pie-making classes in London. My other classes have a fun, Mediterranean vibe, but the pie class is by far the most popular, with Londoners, tourists and people from all over the UK popping in to take part. It proves that the humble pie is still one of the nation's favourite dinners and, of course, it's one of mine, too.

So how did I end up running such a school? I originally left my home, in Cardiff, to form an indie band with my friend, Jayne. I say 'form a band'; it felt more like joining the circus! In the 1990s we did all right (we were local heroes in Wales) and, after moving to London, generated an industry buzz. This led to sold-out singles, packed gigs, an American tour and even a major label deal. We had fun, but split up over musical differences and in separate limos. I soldiered on, writing, producing and performing and then, having discovered Italo disco, I co-ran events on the underground club circuit as well.

Six years ago I finally jumped off the Ferris wheel, the fall thankfully cushioned by another self-discovery: I realised that, despite all the partying and performing, there was a homey side to me, too! Even though I spent so much time writing recipes in between gigs, a career in cooking had never occurred to me but, when it happened, it felt inevitable and completely natural. It was like cooking had been waiting for me all these years but it had allowed me my freedom first.

My mother is my biggest inspiration. As a girl living in Newport, she learned how to cook from the family of an Italian friend. She effortlessly turns her hand to British fare and Mediterranean food and, growing up, I would watch her in the kitchen baking and cooking for hours.

Meanwhile, my father's family are traditional Corfiot cooks. I spent summers in Corfu as a child helping and watching my aunties make trays of stuffed aubergines and peppers using ingredients freshly picked from their farm. We'd bake trays of rich, creamy pastitsio, and I'd help turn the Celebratory Lamb on the spit – I can still smell the lamb, lemon and oregano aromas to this day. My interest in and love of cooking was set, right then and there.

So, I decided to indulge in this new world of food and found that I thoroughly loved it. I began to research the markets (literally!), assist at cookery schools, host supper clubs, I attended a culinary college and eventually became a chef at The Real Greek in Hoxton. I really wanted to teach quality home cooking and, most of all, to instil the confidence to enjoy cooking in all new cooks. With all this behind me, in 2009 I opened Marika's Kitchen, my very own home cookery school that prides itself on its direct, unpretentious approach.

Why pie? When pondering just what defines the ultimate British home cookery course, I kept coming back to the classic pie. People from all walks of life love a good pie: it is comfort and joy all wrapped up in a pastry parcel. I decided right there that it was my calling to teach people the way of the PIE.

I was proved right: it was an immediate hit, from the small classes to mass pie-making clubs in bakeries across London. Of all my cookery classes, my pie class causes the most excitement (and even the odd tear of joy) in people, their faces full of pride as they see their own glorious golden pies rise out of the oven for the first time.

Pies rule! They look good, taste good and you want one right now!

So let's begin.

Introduction

EQUIPMENT FOR PIE-MAKING

Your essential shopping list.

Pie dishes and tins
I love traditional enamel pie dishes, which come in a range of shapes and sizes. Metallic dishes are also good, giving your pie a lovely crisp, evenly browned bottom. Non-stick is third on my list. Unless you cheat and make a pie with just a pastry top, avoid buying ceramic or glass dishes because they are very bad conductors of heat. Measurements tend to be for rectangular dishes, but use whatever you have to hand. As well as pie dishes, I also use muffin and tart tins in the recipes in this book. Muffin tins are of the standard size, and I specify the appropriate dimensions for the tart tins in each recipe.

Kitchen scales
When it comes to baking, to avoid any nasty surprises you must never, ever, guess. Digital scales are more precise, but the spring scale looks nicer and works just as well, especially for larger measurements. I love the retro 1950s look.

Flour shaker
A shaker saves you dipping your hand in the flour packet and making a mess; it also shakes out the right quantity of fine flour; plus, they look great. I have a vintage Home Pride Fred shaker that I love dearly.

Rolling pin
The best rolling pin for pastry, in my opinion, is the humble wooden rolling pin. Some people have had theirs for 30 years and they're still in great shape! Never submerge your pin in the washing-up bowl; simply wipe clean with a damp cloth, dry, and store.

TIP
Dust your work surface and your rolling pin with flour, but avoid flouring your pastry – you don't want to dry it out.

Digital timer
This is an essential tool for pie baking. It's so easy to forget to take your pie out of the oven if you are busy doing something else, and what a shame to over-bake or even burn your lovely pies. Don't rely on egg timers, or even your oven timer. Think of it as your friend; carry it with you while you watch your favourite TV show, waiting for your pie to cook.

Pastry brush
Another essential tool. Egg wash acts as a glue to stick your pie together and, of course, washing or glazing the top will make your pie look beautiful and golden and shiny. Very thin silicone brushes are great because they're easier to wash and last longer than natural bristle brushes.

Cutters of all shapes and sizes
Decorate the top of your pie with leaves, hearts, animals, numbers – anything goes. This is particularly fun when cooking with children.

Small whisk
This is for making the sauce. If you have a non-stick saucepan use a silicone whisk to avoid scraping off the protective layer, otherwise the stainless steel whisk is my favourite.

Baker's hat and white apron
Well, you have to feel and look the part, and I reckon you will perform better if you're suited and booted.

PIE RULES

Master the art of pie with these simple rules.

1. Think cold

Cold fat straight from the fridge, cold fingertips, cold water, work fast and let the dough rest in the fridge for 30 minutes before baking. Hot pastry shrinks in the oven and hot filling poured into a cold pie case will leave you with a soggy bottom. It's the total opposite to bread making when you need warmth, so never knead your pastry, either. See point 6 (overleaf) for more on thinking cold.

2. Think confident

I often find in my classes that people are scared of making pastry! Come on, I bet you have done scarier things in your life than making pastry. Just go for it: you don't need to be an expert pastry chef or a contender for *MasterChef*, you just need a little patience, to follow my easy instructions and to have fun – it's only cooking!

3. Weigh out your ingredients

Why? Baking is a science and, luckily for you, the balancing has already been worked out for you, so you don't need to second-guess. Also, don't heap your spoonfuls when baking. Level your teaspoon or tablespoon measurements (I scrape across the top of the measuring spoon with the flat of my finger or use a straight edge).

4. Do not overwork your pastry

Overworking the gluten in the flour causes your pastry to lose its crumbly texture and become tough and heavy. To avoid this, get in touch with your feminine side (you too, ladies!): be light and airy when making pastry, only the minimal amount of rubbing cold butter into flour is required. I know it's relaxing and feels like playing with sand, but stop it!

Once your pastry has chilled in the fridge, use a one-directional rolling technique to roll it out.

TIP

If your pastry has been in the fridge for much longer than 30 minutes, say 2 hours, or even overnight, rest the pastry on the work surface for 5–10 minutes before rolling so that it can relax and soften.

Sprinkle flour on your work surface, and also on the rolling pin. For every three one-directional rolls, move the pastry a quarter turn and repeat until the pastry is roughly the thickness of a pound coin (about 2mm). Always flour your rolling pin rather than your pastry and keep checking to see if any pieces of pastry have stuck to your pin (if so, just rub them off with your hand and roll again).

Finally, don't stretch your pastry to fit the dish. Push the pastry down to avoid creating air pockets (you can patch up any holes in the pastry with offcuts). Leave an overhang of pastry to tidy up later once the pie is sealed.

5. Reduce the juice in your savoury pie filling

Why? Too much juice and you're risking a soggy bottom, even if the filling is cold. The term 'reduce' just means to thicken the gravy of your pie filling. This mainly applies to casserole type pies like my Classic Steak and Guinness pie on page 68. To achieve this, take the lid off the pot and rapidly heat the mixture so that the liquid evaporates and the sauce thickens. Another trick is to put a tablespoon of flour or cornflour into a small dish, pour over some of the juice from the pot and stir it so that it resembles a thick paste. Pour this paste back into the pot and rapidly reheat – the sauce will soon thicken.

6. Never put hot filling into cold pastry

Why? Because the base of your pie will absorb moisture from the hot filling and it won't cook through, resulting in a soggy bottom. You'll be so disappointed and let down that you might revert to just plonking puff pastry on top of your pies. But by baking your pie with your filling and pastry at the same temperature, you will have a golden, cooked bottom and you'll never doubt your pie-making skills again.

Rembember, think COLD. Cool your mixture down before you put it in your pastry shell. (You could make it the night before and leave it in the fridge so that it has time to cool down completely.)

7. Finish your pie properly (sealing, holes, crimping and glazing)

Every pie deserves to be finished neatly – it will taste better for it, trust me. Egg wash is important – your pie won't hold together without it. To make egg wash, take 1 egg and a teaspoon of cold water and whisk together. Egg-wash around the rim of your pie, place the pastry lid on top and press together to seal. Poke a few holes in the top of your pie to let the steam escape as it cooks, or you can use a ceramic pie bird. (Place the bird in the centre of your filling before you lay the pastry lid over the pie and cut a cross in the pastry lid for him to poke through.) Trim the edge of your pie with a knife and crimp it all the way round using your fingertips or a fork. Glaze the top of your pie with more egg wash for that golden glory moment when your pie comes out of the oven. See pages 22-5 for more instructions on how to finish your pie.

8. Preheat the oven before baking

Don't think, 'Oh well, it won't matter.' It does. If you don't preheat your oven, your pastry will melt and sink on top and you will not achieve your crispy pastry goal. There's no point failing at the last hurdle, so make sure you preheat the oven to the correct temperature before inserting your pie(s). (All ovens vary, so it might be worth investing in an oven thermometer to check the temperature before you start baking.)

To make doubly sure that your pie has a crisp bottom, place a baking tray in the oven while it's preheating and place your pie dish(es) directly on to the heated tray to cook. The blast of heat to the pastry on the bottom will help enormously.

A NOTE ON GLUTEN

Before we make our pastry,
a little science.

Gluten comes from the Latin for
'glue'. It is a protein composite
found in cereal grains that gives
dough the elasticity required to
roll and shape it into your dish.
The pastry will be unmanageable
and crack without at least
some gluten.

However, if too much gluten is
formed it can result in tough
dough. To avoid this, keep
everything cool and keep handling
the dough to a minimum (be
sure to be as quick and light as
possible at each step).

TIP

To help keep excess gluten at
bay, add a dash of apple cider
vinegar or lemon juice to the
cold water (usually a teaspoon or
tablespoon depending on your
recipe). The acidity stalls the
development of gluten, keeping
the crust light and flaky and
lending it a melt-in-the-mouth
texture. This is an especially
useful tip in the summer months
when everything heats faster.

BAKER'S NOTE

For the purposes of this book,
eggs are always large and
preferably free-range; butter is
always salted for savoury pies,
unsalted for sweet pastry; sugar is
caster unless specified otherwise. I
prefer to source my meat from my
local butcher, but just try to get the
best-quality meat you can find.

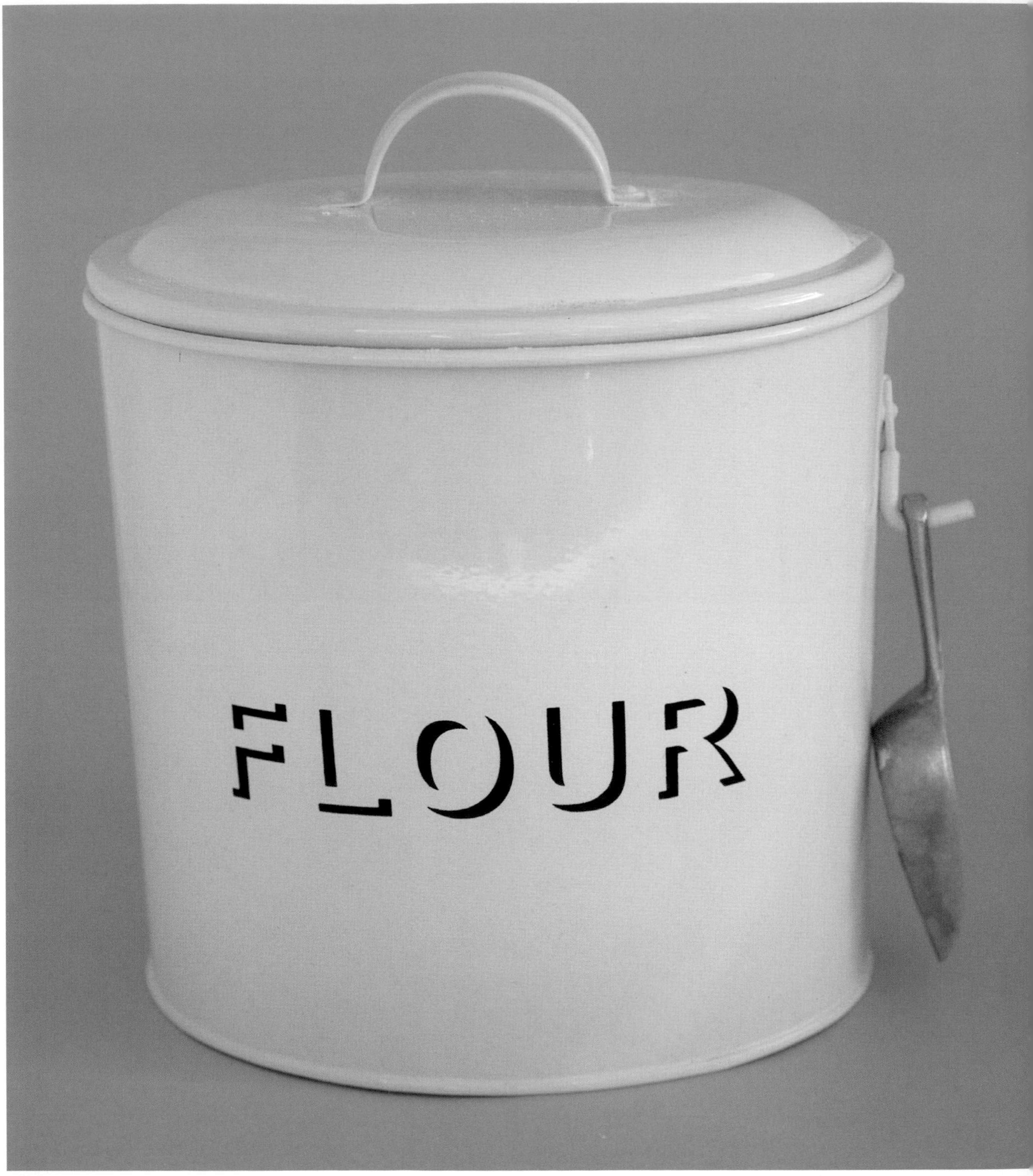
FLOUR

HOW TO MAKE PASTRY

We use shortcrust for most of our pies; rough puff to be a little flash and be able to say, 'Yeah, I can make puff pastry, I don't buy it'; easy tartlet pastry because you will have a soirée from time to time; and flaky pastry for lighter savoury or summer fruit pies.

Note: Some recipes in this book call for their own unique pastry methods so I've included instructions for these on the recipe pages and not in this chapter.

Shortcrust

Ratio of fat to flour: 50%

Shortcrust pastry is the most common pie pastry and the most versatile for sweet and savoury pies, tarts and quiches. It is made with three or four main ingredients: flour, butter (lard or vegetable shortening can also be used depending on the recipe) and water for savoury pastry; flour, butter (or lard or vegetable shortening), water and sugar for sweet pastry – plus a pinch of salt. Its texture is light and crumbly yet robust.

The easiest way to remember how to make shortcrust pastry is to use the half and half method, which is half fat to flour, and half water to butter. For example: 300g flour + 150g butter + 75ml water + a pinch of salt.

TIP

If you fancy something a bit different, blend some sticks of celery or onions in a juicer, sieve and cool in the fridge to use instead of water. This vegetable liquid will give a subtle flavour to your pastry and it's a good way to squeeze in a few more vitamins for the family.

TIP

Also, why not introduce some dried herbs or grated hard cheese to your pastry making – add before the water is mixed in.

HOW TO MAKE SHORTCRUST PASTRY BY HAND

Remember, think COLD: cold hands, cold butter (straight from fridge) and cold water. Refer to the individual recipe for specific measurements.

Step 1. Tip the flour into a mixing bowl with a good pinch of salt. Use a knife to cube the butter and drop it into the flour.

Step 2. Quickly start rubbing the butter and flour together with your fingertips and thumbs, breaking down the lumps until they resemble ground almonds or small breadcrumbs. Lift the flour from the bottom of the mixing bowl to circulate lots of air, and to find more lumps to rub. Go for it: lift it high, mix and let it fall, rubbing as you go.

Step 3. You have to know when to stop. I know it feels lovely, but the more you handle your pastry, the warmer it gets. Think COLD. When most of the lumps of fat have magically disappeared and your mix resembles ground almonds, STOP. Sometimes what you may think are lumps of butter might only be the shortcrust pastry naturally clumping together, so STOP it. Conquer your pastry. You have to control it; don't let it control you.

If you are making sweet pastry, mix in the sugar now.

Step 4. Make a well in the mixture and slowly add the cold water. With one hand holding the side of the bowl steady and the other hand shaped like a claw, make quick circular motions in the flour mix to bring the crumbs together into dough. Don't worry if it's a little crumbly at this stage.

Step 5. Turn out the dough on to a lightly floured surface. Now, with both hands, squeeze the dough together so that all the crumbs merge together. Turn and squeeze, then turn it upside down and squeeze again; try not to handle it too much, just squeeze it all together about six times, until you achieve a lovely smooth dough. If you need a little more moisture, dip your fingertips in cold water and tap them on to the pastry; this should be enough to bring the dough together. Don't add too much water.

Step 6. Once you have a smooth dough, flatten it and wrap it in cling film (flattening the dough instead of forming it into a ball will let in the cool air faster). Place your wrapped dough in the fridge for about 30 minutes to chill.

TIP

REMEMBER THE IMPORTANT PIE RULE: Cool your pie filling right down. If your filling is too hot for your cold pastry you will have an uncooked soggy bottom to your pie, so don't skip this step. I cannot stress this pie rule enough.

HOW TO MAKE SHORTCRUST PASTRY USING A FOOD PROCESSOR

It's all right if you make your shortcrust pastry in the food processor. It's not cheating, it just saves you time and, by using the pulse button, you won't over-handle your pastry (but don't be tempted to press that button too much). The only time you have to be slightly careful is when you add the liquid, so go for it.

Step 1. First check the processor's tool. You need a dough tool, not a blade. Place the flour, cubed butter (or lard or vegetable shortening) and salt into the processor's bowl.

Step 2. Pulse a few times, using the pulse button, until the mixture resembles ground almonds or small breadcrumbs. Don't overwork it. I know it sounds good – just like revving up a motorbike – but restrain yourself.

Step 3. Through the funnel on the top of your processor, slowly add the water, a little at a time, and pulse away until the mixture comes together in a dough ball. Now stop. If you are making sweet pastry, this is the time to add the sugar, ensuring it's well mixed in.

Step 4. Tip out your pastry on to a lightly floured surface and shape it into a rough round. Flatten it, wrap it in cling film and into the fridge it goes for about 30 minutes to chill.

Rough Puff

Ratio of fat to flour: 100%
(bet you never knew that)

Rough puff is a faster, cheat's way to make puff pastry, but it's still effective. Puff pastry is light, crispy and rises in layers as a result of the technique of folding butter into the dough – the butter divides the layers of dough. Puff is used for lighter pies with fish, cheese or sweet fillings, as well as sausage rolls and appetisers.

Step 1. Tip your flour, with a pinch of salt, into a mixing bowl. Use a knife to cube the butter and drop it into the flour.

Step 2. Loosely rub the butter and flour together. You only want to break down the cubes of butter – with puff pastry we want to see lumps of butter in the flour.

Step 3. Make a well in the middle of the mixture and add the cold water, either all at once or half at a time. With one hand holding the side of the bowl and the other hand shaped like a claw, make quick circular motions to bring the mixture together into a firm dough. Flatten the dough, wrap it in cling film and rest it in the fridge for about 20 minutes. (Flattening the dough instead of forming it into a ball will let in the cool air faster.)

Step 4. Lightly flour your work surface, tip your chilled dough on to it and knead briefly, shaping the dough into a rectangle. Flour your rolling pin and roll in one direction, until the dough is three times its original length. You will see a marble effect in the dough. Don't over-roll it and keep the edges straight and even.

Step 5. Fold the bottom third of the dough up to the centre, then fold the top third down over it so that you have a block of folded pastry. Turn the dough a quarter turn (either way) and roll out it out until it is three times the original length. Fold over as before. Wrap the folded dough in cling film and refrigerate for at least 30 minutes before rolling out and using for your pie.

Versatile Tartlet

Ratio of fat to flour: 65%

I call this the easiest pastry in the world. Forget 'blind-baking' (the process of pre-baking a tartlet crust without its filling to ensure a crisp base), this pastry is buttery and crisp already, thanks to the added egg white, and it feels like you're moulding warm play dough into the tins – no fuss.

Step 1. Tip the flour into a mixing bowl with a pinch of salt. Gently melt the butter in a saucepan and pour it into the flour. Take a wooden spoon and mix the flour and butter together. If you're making sweet pastry add the sugar now.

Step 2. Add an egg white and continue to stir until you have a smooth, soft dough. Leave it to rest for a few minutes, then divide into even pieces and roll each piece into a ball. Place one ball in each patty tin hole and press it out to line the tin so that the pastry comes over the edge or, for larger tarts such as the Chocolate, Date and Ginger Tart (see page 100), press the pastry into the base of the tin and up the edges to form a pastry shell. Refrigerate for 30 minutes or pop into the freezer for 5–8 minutes (that's what I do!).

After chilling, the dough shells should feel very firm and cold, ready for filling.

Flaky

Ratio of fat to flour: 65% or 70%

In the US it's all about The Crust! It's an obsession. You hardly ever hear about it in the UK, and I never noticed it until I started checking out how the Americans make their pies. Where we give the recipe for pastry, they give the recipe for 'The Crust'. Flaky pastry gives the crumbliest, flakiest pie crust, perfect for fruit pies. It can be made with or without egg.

Flaky pastry pies like the Apple Huckleberry Three Generations Pie are baked for 15 minutes on a high heat and then lowered for the remainder of the time. Why? The pastry puffs up resulting in a crisp and light flaky pastry, of course. Use a mixture of vegetable shortening (e.g. Crisco, Trex, Cookeen) or lard for texture, and butter for flavour.

Step 1. Add vinegar or lemon juice to ice-cold water (a teaspoon or tablespoon depending on the recipe). If you are adding an egg to the flour and fats, the vinegar or lemon juice can be whisked in with the egg instead.

Step 2. Cube the cold fats and loosely rub together with the flour using your fingertips, leaving pea-sized lumps. (Yes, it's GOOD to leave lumps for this recipe.)

Alternatively, the Delia Smith way is to wrap the fats in foil, freeze them for 45 minutes and simply grate them into the flour, mixing until evenly crumbly. This is a brilliant method and quite easy, too.

Step 3. Next add the ice-cold water mixed with vinegar or lemon juice, and lightly bind together until you have a soft dough. Flatten the dough and wrap it in cling film. Refrigerate for 30 minutes before rolling out and using it to line your pie dish. Refrigerate the dough (in the dish) for 15 minutes before adding the filling.

HOW TO ASSEMBLE AND FINISH YOUR PIE

This is when all the magic comes together, but I don't want you to feel under pressure! It's a very simple process – you just need to learn a few basic techniques. Refer back to my section Pie Rules (see pages 13-14), for more handy tips on achieving pie perfection.

Step 1. When your pastry and filling are completely cool, remove the pastry from the fridge and roll it out to roughly the thickness of a pound coin (about 2mm), using a one-directional rolling technique (see page 13). Remember to flour your rolling pin and worktop and not your pastry, so your pastry doesn't dry out.

Step 2. Don't stretch your pastry to fit the dish. Push the pastry down to avoid air pockets (you can patch up a few holes with leftover pastry). Leave an overhang of pastry to tidy up later once the pie is sealed. Tip your cold pie filling into the pastry-lined dish, then egg-wash all around the rim.

Step 3. Place your pie lid on top and press the edge firmly to seal. Trim the edge with a knife and poke a few holes in the top of the pie to let the steam escape. (If you want to use a pie bird, place it in the centre of your filling before you lay the pastry lid over the pie. Cut a cross in the pastry lid for the pie bird to poke through.)

Step 4. Crimp your pie edge and decorate using one of the methods on pages 24-5, then brush the top of the pie with egg wash, so it will have a lovely shine, and place it on the hot tray in the oven to bake.

CRIMPING AND DECORATING YOUR PIES

PLAITED EDGE

DECORATIVE SHAPES

LATTICE TOP

To make a traditional lattice pie top, use a long ruler and a knife to slice the pastry into roughly 2cm-thick strips. Egg-wash the rim of the pie, then weave the lattice strips across the top, pinching and crimping the edges to keep them tidy. Brush with egg wash. If you're making a sweet pie, you can sprinkle the lattice with sugar.

PINCHING METHOD

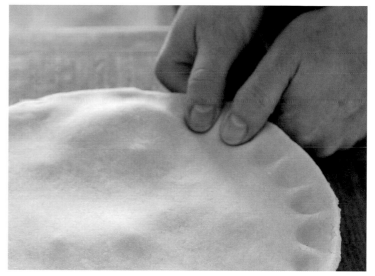

THUMBS

FORK METHOD

KNIFE EDGE

CROSSED CHOPSTICKS

oury
IES

Lamb, Lemon & Oregano Pie

SERVES 4

YOU WILL NEED

25cm x 19cm pie dish

FOR THE FILLING

450g lean lamb, diced
a handful of flour, seasoned
    with 1 tsp black pepper
30g butter
a dash of olive oil
200g shallots, peeled and sliced
a pinch of sugar
1 tsp red wine vinegar
3 garlic cloves, peeled and chopped
2 tbsp dried oregano
juice of 1 lemon
1 chicken stock cube
400ml water
2 waxy potatoes (such as
    Cyprus, Charlotte or Anya),
    peeled and diced
salt and freshly ground black pepper

FOR THE ROUGH PUFF PASTRY

200g plain flour
a pinch of salt
200g butter
90ml cold water, mixed
    with 1 tsp lemon juice

Using the classic lemon and oregano flavours of Greece, my citrusy, fragrant lamb casserole is a delicious meal on its own. When I use it in a pie it only needs a puff pastry lid; any other pastry, or indeed more pastry, would be too heavy for the lightness of these simple fresh flavours. It takes a few hours to make but it's worth the effort.

First make the filling. Lightly coat the lamb in the seasoned flour. Heat half the butter and a dash of olive oil in a frying pan over a high heat. Brown the meat on all sides. Don't add salt at this stage, as it would draw the moisture out and toughen the meat. Set the browned meat aside to rest and release its flavourful juices.

Place a casserole over a medium heat, add the rest of the butter with a dash of olive oil and start to colour the shallots; we want to caramelise them a little so, after 5 minutes, add a pinch of sugar and the vinegar, and stir. Pop the lid on the pot and cook for around 4 minutes, then remove the lid and stir again; the shallots should loosen up and start to change colour.

Recipe continues overleaf

Lamb, Lemon & Oregano Pie CONTINUED

Now add the garlic, oregano, lemon juice, lamb and meat juices to the mix and stir well. Crumble in the stock cube, add the water and mix well to dissolve. Season with salt and pepper. Turn up the heat and bring to the boil, then turn the heat right down and leave to cook slowly for 1–2 hours, checking and stirring occasionally. When it's ready the meat should be tender and the sauce thickened.

Finally, add the potatoes and continue to bubble away with the lid on for 5–7 minutes, until they are cooked through but still firm. If you want a thicker sauce, remove the lid, crank up the heat and allow the liquid to evaporate until you achieve your desired thickness. Leave to cool.

Make the rough puff pastry using the method on page 19.

Once your pastry has chilled for 30 minutes, preheat the oven to 220°C/200°C fan/gas 7.

Assemble your pie using the guidelines on pages 22–5, ensuring both your pastry and filling are cold before assembly.

Place your pie in the oven and bake for 16–20 minutes until puffed and golden.

Serve with a Greek salad and a glass of sparkling wine.

Turkish Breakfast Pie (eaten at lunch) SERVES 6–8

YOU WILL NEED

25cm-round pie dish

FOR THE FILLING

2 small peppers (red and green),
    de-seeded and diced
1 onion, peeled and diced
olive oil, for frying
1 tsp red chilli flakes
½ tsp dried mint
¼ tsp ground cinnamon
juice of ½ lemon
a large handful of roughly chopped
    fresh parsley
3 tbsp passata or 2 tbsp tomato purée
    mixed with 1 tbsp water
10 black olives, pitted and sliced
1 tbsp flour
100g Sucuk sausage (available in
    Halal/Turkish/Cypriot shops or
    online), skinned and sliced
4 eggs
100g feta cheese
optional: a sprinkling of onion
    or nigella seeds
salt and freshly ground black pepper

FOR THE FLAKY PASTRY

100ml ice-cold water
1 tsp lemon juice
100g butter
100g lard or vegetable shortening
    (e.g. Crisco, Trex, Cookeen)
300g plain flour
a pinch of salt
1 egg, whisked with 1 tsp cold
    water, for glazing

This is my Anglo-Turkish breakfast pie. I live a breath away from Green Lanes, in London, where there is a large Turkish community, so I am greeted on a daily basis with the smells and wonderful ideas from the Mediterranean. Many a hungover morning, my partner Clive and I would go and have a Turkish breakfast, and the freshness of the salad, the saltiness of the feta and Sucuk (dry-cured spicy beef sausage) with the eggs, peppers and warm bread would always hit the spot. I use flaky pasty for this pie because its light and crispy crust can handle the strong flavours and robust filling.

Recipe continues overleaf

Turkish Breakfast Pie (eaten at lunch) CONTINUED

First prepare the filling. In a saucepan over a medium heat, fry the peppers and onions in a little olive oil for about 6 minutes, until softened. Add the chilli flakes, mint, cinnamon, lemon juice, parsley and a good pinch of salt and pepper, and continue to fry for a few minutes. Next add the passata and olives. Turn off the heat, stir in the flour and leave to cool completely.

In a hot, dry frying pan, fry the slices of Sucuk for 1 minute on each side. Set aside for later.

Make the flaky pastry using the method on page 20.

Once you've returned the pastry to the fridge for the second time, preheat the oven to 220°C/200°C fan/gas 7 and place a baking tray inside to heat up.

Assemble your pie using the guidelines on pages 22–5, ensuring both your pastry and filling are cold before assembly. Once you have filled your pastry shell, crack 4 eggs on top (try to space them evenly so each quarter will include an egg) and dot slices of Sucuk and crumbled feta around them. Then seal the pie with a pastry lid, egg-wash the top and finish by sprinkling with onion or nigella seeds, if using.

Place your pie on the hot tray in the oven and bake for 15 minutes, then reduce the oven temperature to 200°C/180°C fan/gas 6 and bake for a further 25–30 minutes until golden brown.

Serve with a tomato and cucumber salad.

Spinach and Dill Greek Fried Pies

MAKES ABOUT 20 LITTLE PIES

YOU WILL NEED
8.5cm-round pastry or biscuit cutter
(or use the rim of a large glass)

FOR THE FILLING
olive oil
5 spring onions, roughly chopped
(use the green bits, too)
500g fresh spinach leaves (preferably
with large leaves, and use the stems),
washed, drained and chopped
50g roughly chopped fresh dill
¼ tsp dried mint, or use 6 fresh leaves,
roughly chopped
a good squeeze of lemon juice
½ tsp salt
½ tsp freshly ground black pepper
grated zest of ½ lemon
25g grated hard cheese (like Parmesan
or a hard goats' cheese)

FOR THE OLIVE OIL PASTRY
250g plain flour
1 tsp salt
2 tbsp olive oil
2 tbsp lemon juice
100ml cold water
vegetable oil, for deep-frying

Greeks mainly use olive oil in their pastry instead of butter (if they are not using filo sheets for a typical Greek recipe, such as spinach and feta pie). The olive oil makes the pastry more robust and good to chew on. My little fried pies are filled with 'goodness greens' and, surprisingly, are not greasy at all. They are simple to make and perfect for gatherings. Eat them warm, served with thick Greek yoghurt and lemon wedges.

First prepare the filling. Put a splash of olive oil into a pan over a medium heat and fry the spring onions for a few minutes, until soft. Add the spinach, dill, mint and lemon juice, season with the salt and pepper and continue to fry for a further 5 minutes.

Sieve the mixture to drain off the liquid. Next fold through the lemon zest and cheese. Leave to cool completely in the sieve so that any extra drops of liquid can escape. (You don't want soggy pies.)

Meanwhile make the pastry. Put the flour and salt in a mixing bowl, make a well in the centre and add the oil and lemon juice. Mix well. Add the water, a little at a time, with one hand binding and kneading slightly as you pour, until you have smooth dough. You might not need to use all the water. Roll the dough into a ball, wrap in cling film and pop it into the fridge to chill for 30 minutes.

Recipe continues overleaf

Spinach and Dill Greek Fried Pies CONTINUED

Now prepare your pies. Once your dough has chilled, roll it out to a thin sheet (as thin as you can get it). Cut out round shapes with the cutter and spoon 1 tablespoon of mixture on to each circle, off-centre. Fold the circles over to make half-moon shapes and press the edges together to seal. Don't worry if you think the pastry is tough, it's meant to be.

Pour the vegetable oil into a deep-sided pan to a depth of 8–10cm. Turn on the heat to medium-high and heat the oil until a cube of bread dropped into the hot oil sizzles and turns golden within a few seconds.

Using a slotted spoon, carefully drop 2 or 3 little pies into the oil. Fry until golden brown on both sides – they will only take a few minutes. Remove from the pan and drain on kitchen roll until crispy and dry. Repeat until all the pies are cooked.

Mum's Red Salmon and Caper Plaited Pie

SERVES 4–5

FOR THE FILLING
1 x 420g tin of red salmon or wild
    Pacific pink salmon
a handful of capers
a good grind of black pepper
1 tsp chopped fresh dill
1½ tbsp light mayonnaise

FOR THE PUFF PASTRY
320g home-made rough puff
    pastry (see page 19) or shop-bought,
    ready-rolled puff pastry
a sprinkling of flour
1 egg, whisked with 1 tsp cold water,
    for glazing
a sprinkling of onion or poppy seeds

This is my mum's fast summer pie so I had to include it for busy mums (and pie lovers) everywhere. From start to plate it takes just 30 minutes. It actually looks more like a very large plaited sausage roll.

Preheat the oven to 200°C/180°C fan/gas 6. Lay a sheet of baking parchment over a baking tray.

Prepare your filling. Clear all the skin and bones from the salmon and mix it together with the rest of the filling ingredients. Set aside.

Lay out your pastry sheet. If your pastry has been pre-rolled for you, just dust the surface with a little flour and give it a couple of extra rolls with a rolling pin to shape it up. If you're using home-made roll out to a rectangle approximately 3mm thick. Transfer your pastry to the baking tray.

Make the plaits by cutting 5cm-wide strips with a sharp knife, slicing away from the filling, making sure the slits are evenly spaced on either side.

Now it's time to assemble your pie. Spoon the salmon filling in a line down the centre of the pastry sheet, as if you're making a large sausage roll.

Fold over the top and bottom ends of the pastry and, starting at one end, cross the first pastry strips diagonally across the filling. Take the top strip from the other side and cross that over the first strip already on the filling. (see photograph, overleaf). Continue plaiting the strips in this way, folding in the loose ends as you go, until you have a neat plaited sausage shape. Egg-wash the top of the pie and sprinkle over some seeds.

Bake in the hot oven for 18–20 minutes until the pastry has puffed up and turned golden brown. Slice and serve it on a hot summer's day with a massive salad.

Mediterranean Tartlets

MAKES 12 MINI TARTLETS

YOU WILL NEED
*12-hole patty tin, or impress with
a 36cm x 12cm x 3cm tart tin*

FOR YOUR VERSATILE TARTLET PASTRY
*180g plain flour
a pinch of salt
100g butter
1 egg white*

FOR THE FILLING
*100ml double cream
3 egg yolks
¼ tsp hot paprika
10 capers, roughly chopped,
   or 5 anchovies, sliced
2 tsp dried oregano
6 sundried tomatoes, rehydrated
   in a little water (no need to
   rehydrate if stored in oil)
120g feta cheese*

I make a batch of these every time there is a party or a small gathering. They are very simple and I like having a reliable card up my sleeve for any occasion. Eaten hot or cold, you can even make them the day before to save you time. You can vary the filling, as long as you keep the same measurements of cream and egg yolks; for example you could use 120g cream cheese with flakes of smoked salmon and capers. Experiment.

First make the versatile tartlet pastry and line your tray(s) using the method on page 20.

Preheat the oven to 200°C/180°C fan/gas 6.

Prepare the filling. In a mixing bowl whisk together the cream and egg yolks, until slightly thickened. Whisk in the paprika, then mix in the capers, oregano, drained tomatoes and crumble in the feta (remember the feta and capers are salty, so no need to add salt).

Once your pastry case(s) have chilled for 30 minutes, spoon in the cold filling and cook in the centre of the oven, until golden brown and the centre is bouncy. This will take 18–20 minutes for tartlets or 25 minutes for a single large tart.

Cheese and Red Onion Pasties

MAKES 12 LITTLE PASTIES

YOU WILL NEED
11.5cm-round pastry or biscuit cutter

FOR THE ROUGH PUFF PASTRY
150g plain flour, plus extra to dust
a pinch of salt
150g butter
70ml cold water mixed with
*   1 tsp lemon juice*
1 egg, whisked with 1 tsp cold water,
*   for glazing*

FOR THE FILLING
60g mashed potato
170g mature Cheddar cheese,
*   crumbled (not grated)*
½ red onion, peeled and
*   finely chopped*
¼ tsp ground nutmeg
¼ tsp mild smoked paprika
¼ tsp onion seeds

These little pasties are serious pleasure bombs! They are the first to go at any gathering; the nutmeg, onion seeds and paprika making everyone's taste buds sing. No one will believe you made the pastry though, because no one makes puff pastry, right? Wrong. You can, and it's simple, too. Serve with a little Branston pickle.

First make the rough puff pastry using the method on page 19 (or you can cheat and buy some from the shop).

Then make the filling. In a bowl, mix together the potato, Cheddar, onion, spices and onion seeds.

Preheat the oven to 220°C/200°C fan/gas 7. Line a baking tray with baking parchment.

Shape the pasties. Roll out your pastry on a lightly floured surface to the thickness of a pound coin (about 2mm). Use your cutter to mark out 12 circles. Place a tablespoon of the cheese mixture in the centre of each pastry circle, brush around the edge of the circle with whisked egg, fold into half-moons and seal. Crimp along the edges using a fork and prick each pasty top so that the steam can escape as it cooks. Lay them on the lined baking tray (not too close together) and lightly brush the tops with more egg wash.

Bake in the preheated oven for 15 minutes. Cool a little on a wire rack, then serve with a little pickle and watch how they fly off the plate!

Minute Picnic Pasties MAKES 12–14

YOU WILL NEED
11.5cm-round pastry or biscuit cutter

FOR THE FILLING
olive oil
1 stick of celery
½ large carrot
½ sweet potato
½ yellow or red pepper
8 green beans
1 garlic clove, peeled and sliced
1 tsp hot paprika
1 tsp crushed coriander seeds
zest of ½ lemon
salt and freshly ground black pepper

FOR THE PASTY PASTRY
250g plain or wholemeal flour,
  plus extra to dust
50g grated Parmesan cheese
1 tsp salt
2 tbsp olive oil
2 tsp butter, melted
60ml cold water
1 egg, whisked with 1 tsp cold water,
  for glazing

These tiny treats are best eaten outside at a picnic, holding them only between forefinger and thumb, and nibbling like a dainty, delicate, annoying person. You could lightly dip them into crème fraîche or lemon mayonnaise, or you could wolf them down under the picnic blanket because they are so naughtily moreish that you can't bear to share!

Preheat the oven to 200°C/180°C fan/gas 6.

First prepare the filling. Rinse, peel and finely dice all the vegetables (remember they are going into mini pastry parcels so keep them small). Arrange the diced vegetables and the garlic on a roasting tray. Drizzle with a good glug of olive oil, season with salt and pepper, then sprinkle over the paprika and coriander seeds. Roast for 15 minutes. Transfer the veggies to a bowl, add the lemon zest and leave to cool.

Next make the pasty pastry. Put the flour, Parmesan and salt in a bowl with the oil and melted butter. Rub the fats into the flour, then make a well in the centre and pour in the

water, a little at a time, binding the pastry together with your fingers until you have a dough. Wrap in cling film and pop into the fridge for 30 minutes until you are ready to roll.

When you're ready to bake, preheat the oven to 200°C/180°C fan/gas 6. Dust a baking tray with flour.

Now assemble your pasties. Roll out the pastry thinly on a floured surface. (This pastry is tough, so use your strength.) Use a pastry cutter to cut out a circle, add a tablespoon of the cool filling just off-centre, then dampen the edge with a little water using a pastry brush. Carefully fold over the pastry to make a half-moon shape. Dab a fork in some flour and press it down along the pastry edge to seal, then pierce the top of the pie with a fork once so that air can escape. Repeat until you've used up all your pastry and filling. Transfer your pasties to the baking tray.

Bake for 10 minutes, then remove from the oven, brush over the tops with the egg wash and return them to the oven to bake for a further 10 minutes. Cool on a wire rack.

Porky Pies

MAKES 12 LITTLE PIES

YOU WILL NEED
12-hole muffin tray
8.5cm-round pastry or biscuit cutter

FOR THE FILLING
a bunch of spring onions, finely
* chopped (use the green bits too)*
a handful of finely chopped
* fresh parsley*
butter, for frying
5 pork sausages, split and
* meat removed*
100g unsmoked bacon rashers (include
* a little of the fat), roughly chopped*
½ tsp ground nutmeg
½ tsp ground allspice
½ tsp pimentón (smoked hot paprika)
salt and freshly ground black pepper

FOR THE HOT-WATER CRUST PASTRY
500g plain flour, plus extra for dusting
1 tsp salt
50ml water
50ml milk
150g non-hydrogenated lard
1 egg, whisked with 1 tbsp cold water,
* for glazing*

My family were visiting one Mother's Day and I wanted to bake something special. Now, I know it's a strange choice, but my mum loves a good pork pie. However, I wanted to make an easier filling using good butcher's sausages, bacon and spices. The pastry is a classic hot-water crust made with non-hydrogenated lard (better for you than vegetable shortening), which takes minutes to make. These little pies make a super supper with some pickles and mustard. Traditional pastry, not so traditional filling, so I name them Porky Pies.

First make the filling. Fry the spring onions and the parsley in a large knob of butter over a medium heat for 3 minutes. Transfer to a mixing bowl and leave to cool. Add the sausage meat and chopped bacon rashers, the spices, a good grind of pepper and a pinch of salt. Mix it all together with your hands and set aside to cool.

Preheat the oven to 180°C /160°C fan/gas 4 and place a baking tray inside to heat up. Lightly grease the muffin tray.

Now make the pastry. Tip the flour and salt into a mixing bowl. In a pan over a low heat, gently heat the water, milk and lard until the lard has melted. Make a well in the flour and pour in all the lard mixture. With one hand, work quickly to combine the fats and the flour until a rough dough forms. Turn out on to a lightly floured surface and squeeze together to form a smooth dough (you will have to do a little kneading).

Recipe continues overleaf

Porky Pies

Divide the dough into 4 pieces and roll out one piece to roughly the thickness of a pound coin (about 2mm). Use a larger cutter to cut out as many pastry bases as you can. This pastry has a warm play dough feel so you can easily mould it into each muffin shell. Push the pastry right to the bottom to ensure there are no air bubbles and leave a small overhang. Repeat, rolling out more pastry as necessary until all of your pie bases are made.

Now assemble your pies. Tightly pack the meat filling into each pastry shell. Roll out the remaining dough and use a small cutter to cut out the pie tops (you can make these a lot thinner, too). Brush the edges with the egg wash and pop the tops on, pinching up the sides to seal the pies. Cut out a little hole in the top of each pie to let the steam escape, and finally egg-wash them.

Place your muffin tray on the hot tray in the oven and bake for 30 minutes. Remove from the oven and let the pies cool a little before removing each one (using a palette knife to loosen the edges) and transferring them directly on to the hot baking tray. Return to the oven for a further 20 minutes to crisp up the bottoms and edges. Leave to cool completely on a wire rack before eating.

Waldorf (Salad) Summer Pies

MAKES 6 INDIVIDUAL HANDHELD PIES

YOU WILL NEED
6-hole non-stick deep muffin tray

FOR THE SAUCE
25g butter
25g flour
250ml milk
1½ tbsp Dijon mustard
½ tsp white wine vinegar
   or apple cider vinegar
salt and freshly ground black pepper

FOR THE FILLING
150g waxy potatoes (such as Cyprus,
Charlotte or Anya), peeled
   and medium diced
a bunch of spring onions, trimmed
   and chopped
2 sticks of celery, chopped
1 garlic clove, peeled and finely
   chopped
olive oil, for frying
1 red apple (such as Braeburn or Cox's),
   peeled and finely sliced
50g walnuts, roughly chopped
30g raisins
50g watercress or rocket
zest of ½ lemon and 1 tbsp juice
salt

FOR THE
SHORTCRUST PASTRY
300g plain flour
a pinch of salt
75g butter
75g vegetable shortening
   (e.g. Crisco, Trex, Cookeen)
25g grated Parmesan or
   other hard cheese
75ml cold water mixed with
   1 tsp apple cider vinegar

This is a take on the classic Waldorf salad, which, with the addition of waxy potatoes, a Dijon mustard sauce, plus a few other tweaks, works really well as a pie filling. Each bite has a different refreshing taste, with the crisp crunchiness of the apples and walnuts, fragrant lemon zest, sweet raisins, the satisfying body of the potatoes, the tangy kick of the sauce and finally, the shortcrust pastry . . . need I go on? Make this for a real summer veggie treat.

Recipe continues overleaf

Waldorf (Salad) Summer Pies CONTINUED

First make the sauce. Melt the butter in a saucepan over a low heat. Once melted, whisk in the flour until you have a smooth paste (known as a roux). Add the milk, all at once, and whisk continuously for a few minutes. When the sauce starts to thicken, take the saucepan off the heat, add the mustard and vinegar and season with salt and pepper, continuing to whisk. Once all the ingredients are well combined, set aside to cool.

Now make the filling. Bring a small saucepan of salted water to the boil and parboil the potatoes for 6 minutes.

Meanwhile, fry the spring onions, celery and garlic in olive oil for a few minutes, until softened. Drain the potatoes and add them to the mix. Continue to fry until the potatoes are slightly browned. Add a good pinch of salt. If the ingredients look dry, add 2 tablespoons of water and stir to loosen up the flavours. Leave to cool completely.

Once the potato mixture is cool, mix it together with the remaining filling ingredients and set aside while you make your pastry.

Make the shortcrust pastry using one of the methods on page 17–19.

Once your pastry has chilled for 30 minutes, preheat the oven to 200°C/180°C fan/gas 6.

Assemble your pies using the guidelines on page 22–25, ensuring both your pastry and filling are cold before assembly.

Place your muffin tray on the hot tray in the oven and bake for 30 minutes until golden brown. Cool slightly on a wire rack before serving with a Pimm's drinkie on a summer's day.

Gammon Country Pies

MAKES 8 HANDHELD PIES OR 2 X 20CM-ROUND PIES

YOU WILL NEED

2 x 6-hole non-stick deep
   muffin trays or 2 x 20cm-round
   pie dishes
Suggestion: bake one and freeze one
   for another day (see page 103 for
   tips on freezing)

FOR THE SAUCE

20g butter
20g cornflour
300ml full-fat milk
1 tsp mustard
100g grated mature or medium
   Cheddar cheese
½ tsp salt
½ tsp freshly ground black pepper

FOR THE FILLING

olive oil, for frying
2 onions, peeled and sliced
500g unsmoked gammon
   or bacon, diced
300g potatoes, peeled and diced
1 garlic clove, peeled and crushed
2 large or 3 small courgettes, diced
a good grind of black pepper
1 tsp dried or fresh tarragon

TIP

Don't add any salt to the mixture,
as the gammon will give enough.

FOR THE SHORTCRUST PASTRY

500g plain flour
a pinch of salt
250g butter
125ml cold water
1 egg, whisked with 1 tsp cold water,
   for egg-washing and glazing

I am a city girl at heart, but if I were to live in the country this would be my dream country pie, full of chunky, simple ingredients picked from the land, enjoyed with a glass of ale. I have made this pie quite a lot because the creamy cheese sauce with the gammon and potatoes is a wonderful thing.

First make the sauce. Melt the butter in a saucepan over a low heat. Once melted, whisk in the cornflour until you have a smooth paste (known as a roux). Add the milk, all at once, and whisk continuously for a few minutes. When the sauce starts to thicken, take the saucepan off the heat, add the mustard and cheese and season with the salt and pepper, continuing to whisk. Once all the ingredients are well combined, set aside to cool.

Now make the filling. Pour a good glug of olive oil into a deep-sided saucepan or casserole set over a medium heat. Add the onions and fry for 5 minutes, then add the gammon and potatoes and fry for a further 5 minutes, until brown on all sides.

Next add the garlic, courgettes, a grind of pepper and the tarragon. Stir and cook for a further 8–10 minutes. Turn off the heat and leave to cool slightly on the hob. Stir the rested sauce into the filling mixture and leave to cool completely.

Make the shortcrust pastry using the method on pages 17–19.

Once your pastry has chilled for 30 minutes, preheat the oven to 200°C/180°C fan/gas 6 and place 2 baking trays inside to heat up.

Assemble your pies using the guidelines on pages 22–25, ensuring both your pastry and filling are cold before assembly. Try cutting out farm animal shapes for decoration, egg-washing them in place, and crimp the edges of your pies.

Place your pies on the hot trays in the oven and bake for 25–30 minutes for individual pies or 30–40 minutes for large pies, until they are golden brown.

Serve with pickles and a glass of ale.

Italian Sausage and Pesto Sauce Pie

SERVES 4

YOU WILL NEED
25cm x 19cm pie dish

FOR THE SAUCE
10g butter
10g plain flour
150ml milk
2 level tbsp green pesto
salt and freshly ground black pepper

FOR THE FILLING
2 leeks, trimmed and roughly sliced
200g waxy potatoes (such as Cyprus, Charlotte or Anya), peeled and diced
olive oil, for frying
4 pork and fennel sausages (preferably Italian), split and meat removed
100g mushrooms (chestnut or medium portobello), sliced
a knob of butter
1 tsp grated lemon zest
salt and freshly ground black pepper

FOR THE SHORTCRUST PASTRY
300g plain flour
a pinch of salt
150g butter
75ml cold water
1 egg, whisked with 1 tsp cold water, for egg-washing and glazing

This pie was inspired by a gorgeous meal I had at my friends Raff and Spiro's home (Raff is Italian and Spiro is Greek). Raff, being a true Italian cook, had made the pesto from scratch and brought over the sausages, olive oil (both made at her family home), pasta and Parmesan from Italy. As you can imagine, with its authentic ingredients, it tasted divine. One day, looking at a half-used jar of pesto in my fridge, I thought I would try to make a pie version, without the pasta and with a few additional, complementary ingredients. And you know what? It really does work!

If you can't find pork and fennel sausages, buy pork and add half a teaspoon of fennel seeds. I buy my sausages from a good butcher because they have a high meat content. Try to buy the best quality you can find. A sign of a bad sausage is when you fry them and lots of water and fat is released.

Recipe continues overleaf

Italian Sausage and Pesto Sauce Pie CONTINUED

First make the sauce. Melt the butter in a small saucepan over a medium-high heat. Add the flour and whisk well for a few minutes until you have a smooth paste (known as a roux). Next add all the milk at once, whisking continuously until the sauce starts to thicken. Now take the saucepan off the heat, add the pesto, a little salt and pepper, mix and leave to cool.

Then make the filling. First prepare the leeks. Bring a large pan of salted water to the boil. Half-fill a bowl with cold water and set aside. Tip the sliced leeks into the pan of boiling salted water and cook for 4 minutes, then drain in a colander and tip into the bowl of cold water. Leave for a couple of minutes and then drain again. This method retains the colour, nutrients and flavour of the leeks. Squeeze the excess water from the leeks and leave them in the colander until you need them.

Place a deep-sided frying pan or wok over a high heat and sauté the diced potatoes in olive oil until they brown a little. Break up the sausage meat into little chunks and fry with the potatoes for about 8 minutes, until the sausage meat starts to brown. (If you're using fennel seeds to impart flavour to pork sausages, add them now.)

Add the sliced mushrooms and a knob of butter and fry until the mushrooms have shrunk to half their size. Next add the lemon zest and a pinch of salt and pepper. Set aside to cool completely.

TIP

To speed up the cooling process, transfer the filling from the hot pan to a chilled bowl, mix in the sauce and leeks and set aside to cool completely.

Make the shortcrust pastry using one of the methods on pages 17–19.

Once your pastry has chilled for 30 minutes, preheat the oven to 200°C/180°C fan/gas 6 and place a baking tray inside to heat up.

Assemble your pie using the guidelines on pages 22–25, ensuring both your pastry and filling are cold before assembly.

Place your pie on the hot tray in the oven and bake for 30 minutes until golden brown. This pie is best served warm with a tomato and basil salad.

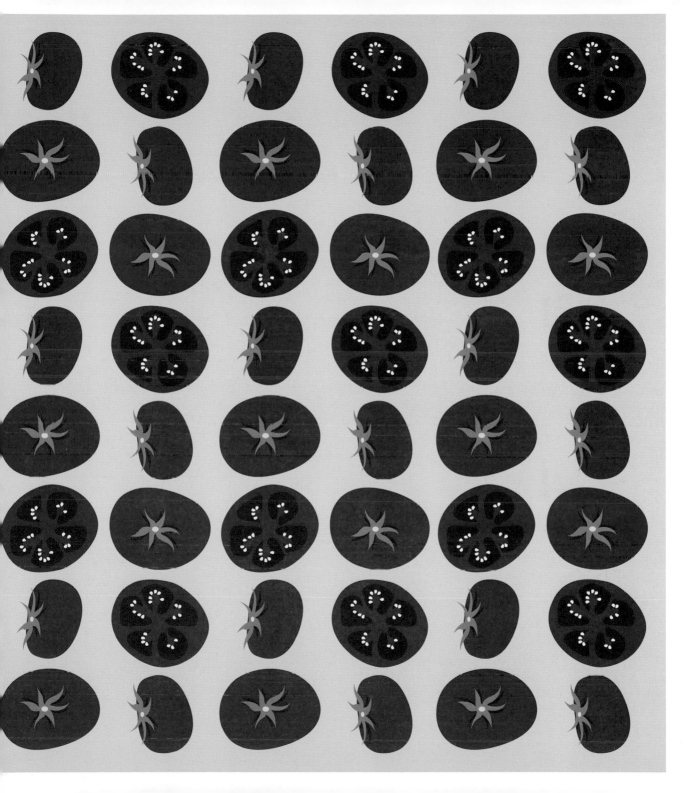

Cambridge Huntingdon Fidget Pies

MAKES 8 HANDHELD PIES

YOU WILL NEED
2 x 6-hole non-stick deep muffin trays

FOR THE FILLING
30g butter
1 onion, peeled and finely chopped
*1 potato, approx. 300g once peeled
    and diced*
1 tbsp plain flour
*400g unsmoked back gammon,
    fat and rind removed*
*1 cooking apple, approx. 300g once
    cored, peeled and diced*
*1 heaped tbsp finely chopped
    fresh parsley*
*1 heaped tbsp finely chopped
    fresh sage*
1 bay leaf
250ml cider
salt and freshly ground black pepper

FOR THE SHORTCRUST PASTRY
500g plain flour
a pinch of salt
125g lard (or vegetable shortening)
125g butter
125ml cold water
*1 egg, whisked with 1 tsp cold water,
    for egg-washing and glazing*

I had never heard of these little pies before I was asked to teach a pie class for the Cambridge Society. They weren't originally made to sell to the public, but instead were baked to feed the hard workers at harvest festival time in the eighteenth century. 'Fidget' comes from the word 'fitchet', which is slang for polecat; it was said that the smell the pies emitted while they cooked reminded cooks of the smell of polecats. Hmm, odd, but don't let that put you off: this is an insanely satisfying pie, actually one of my new favourites. Reworking a classic recipe was a pleasure.

First make the filling. Heat the butter in a frying pan over a medium heat. Cook the onions until soft, then tip in the diced potatoes and flour. Stir well and continue to cook for 5 minutes until the potatoes have slightly browned.

Add the bacon to the pan and fry until the potatoes start to soften. Add the apple and herbs and season with lots of ground black pepper and a pinch of salt.

Next add the cider, bring to a simmer, then turn the heat down to low and let simmer for 10 minutes, stirring every few minutes. (Avoid stirring too much.)

After 10 minutes the cider should have formed a thick gravy, coating all the ingredients. If it is still a little thin, simmer for a bit longer on a higher heat until the juices have reduced. Set aside the filling to cool completely.

Make the shortcrust pastry using one of the methods on pages 17–19.

Once your pastry has chilled for 30 minutes, preheat the oven to 200°C/180°C fan/gas 6.

Assemble your pies using the guidelines on page 22, ensuring both your pastry and filling are cold before assembly.

Place your muffin trays on the hot tray in the oven and bake for 30 minutes until golden brown, checking after 25 minutes to make sure they're not burning.

Transfer your fidget pies to a wire rack to cool slightly, then devour them with a glass of cider.

Butternut Squash and Leek Pie SERVES 8

YOU WILL NEED:
20cm– or 22cm–round pie dish

FOR THE FILLING
500g butternut squash, peeled,
    de-seeded and diced
200g carrots, peeled and diced
4 garlic cloves (whole and unpeeled)
olive oil
2 leeks (use the green leaves too),
    sliced
350ml milk
a good handful of finely chopped
    fresh mint leaves
100g frozen peas
½ tsp cayenne pepper
salt

FOR THE SAUCE
25g butter
25g flour or cornflour
1½ tsp vegetable bouillon
the reserved milk from
    poaching the leeks
1 tsp mustard
30g grated Parmesan
    or other hard cheese
salt and freshly ground pepper

FOR THE FLAKY PASTRY
100ml ice-cold water
1 tsp lemon juice
100g butter
100g vegetable shortening
    (e.g. Crisco, Trex, Cookeen)
300g plain flour
a pinch of salt
1 egg, whisked with 1 tsp
    cold water, for glazing

This is a very fresh-tasting pie. The filling is quite light, so tucking into the crispy flaky pastry shell provides a lovely marriage of textures. Serve as a cold summer pie, with minted peas.

Preheat the oven to 200°C/180°C fan/gas 6 and grease a baking tray.

First make the filling. Lay the squash and carrots on the greased baking tray. Scatter the garlic cloves (in their skins) around the squash, drizzle with a little olive oil, season with salt and toss to coat. Bake in the hot oven for 15 minutes.

Put the sliced leeks in a saucepan over a low heat with the milk and a pinch of salt. Poach for 15 minutes, then sieve the leeks, squeezing out the excess milk and reserving the milk for the sauce. Transfer the leeks to a large bowl with the mint and set aside to cool.

Recipe continues overleaf

Butternut Squash and Leek Pie CONTINUED

When the squash and carrots have cooked for 15 minutes, take them out of the oven and add them to the bowl with the leeks. Squeeze out the garlic from their skins and add to the bowl with the frozen peas, a little salt and the cayenne pepper. Mix to combine.

Now make the sauce. Melt the butter in a saucepan over a low heat. Once melted, whisk in the flour or cornflour and bouillon until you have a smooth paste (known as a roux). Add the reserved milk, all at once, and whisk continuously for a few minutes. When the sauce starts to thicken, take the saucepan off the heat, add the mustard and cheese and season with salt and pepper, continuing to whisk. Once all the ingredients are well combined, pour the sauce into the butternut squash mix and leave to cool completely.

Make the flaky pastry using the method on page 20.

Once you've returned the pastry to the fridge for the second time, preheat the oven to 220°C/200°C fan/gas 7 and place a baking tray inside to heat up.

Assemble your pie using the guidelines on pages 22–25, ensuring both your pastry and filling are cold before assembly.

Place your pie on the hot tray in the oven and bake for 15 minutes, then reduce the heat to 200°C/180°C fan/gas 6 and bake for a further 25 minutes until golden brown on top. Leave to cool completely and serve with refreshing minted peas.

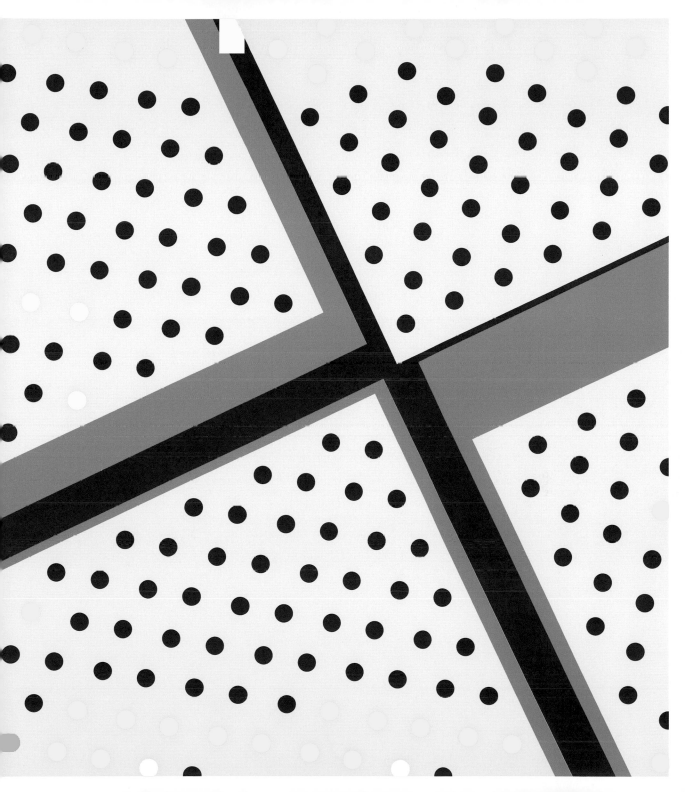

Classic Chicken, Leek and Bacon Pie

MAKES 8 HANDHELD PIES OR 2 LARGE PIES

YOU WILL NEED

*2 x 6-hole non-stick deep muffin trays
or 2 x 20cm-round pie dishes
Suggestion: bake one and freeze
one for another day (see page 103
for tips on freezing)*

FOR THE WHITE SAUCE

*30g butter
30g flour
350ml milk
2 tsp mustard
½ chicken stock cube
salt and freshly ground black pepper*

FOR THE FILLING

*olive oil, for frying
600g chicken, diced into
bite-sized pieces
a knob of butter
1 leek, trimmed and sliced
1 onion, peeled and diced
100g lardons or smoked streaky
bacon, diced
100g mushrooms, chopped
2 garlic cloves, peeled and sliced
1 tsp dried tarragon or sage
salt and freshly ground black pepper*

FOR THE SHORTCRUST PASTRY

*500g plain flour
a pinch of salt
250g butter
40g grated Parmesan cheese
125ml cold water
1 egg, whisked with 1 tsp cold water,
for egg-washing and glazing*

There is no messing with the classic combination of flavours in this pie, which is always a winner and a favourite in my classes. What's not to love? It has a creamy sauce with a mustard kick, chicken, smoky bacon and the unique flavour of Welsh leek. Lush! Simply devour on its own.

First make the sauce. Melt the butter in a saucepan over a low heat. Once melted, whisk in the flour until you have a smooth paste (known as a roux). Add the milk, all at once, and whisk continuously for a few minutes. When the sauce starts to thicken, take the saucepan off the heat, add the mustard, crumble in the stock cube and season with salt and pepper, continuing to whisk. Once all the ingredients are well combined, set aside to cool.

Now make the filling. Heat some olive oil in a casserole dish over a medium heat and seal the diced chicken on all sides for about 5 minutes, until slightly browned. Don't add salt at this stage, as it will draw out the moisture from the chicken, but give it a good sprinkling of pepper. Remove the chicken from the pan and set aside in a dish to release its juices.

Keeping the casserole on the heat, add a little butter and fry the leek and onion until they are shiny. Add the lardons or bacon and mushrooms and fry for a few minutes until the bacon is browned and the mushrooms have reduced in size by about half. Season with salt and pepper. Finally add the garlic and tarragon or sage. Tip the chicken and its rested juices back into the pan, stir and cook for a further 5 minutes. Turn off the heat, stir in the sauce and leave to cool completely.

Make the shortcrust pastry using the method on pages 17–19.

Once your pastry has chilled for 30 minutes, preheat the oven to 200°C/180°C fan/gas 6 and place 2 baking trays inside to heat up.

Assemble your pies using the guidelines on pages 22–25, ensuring both your pastry and filling are cold before assembly.

Place your pies on the hot trays in the oven and bake for 25–30 minutes for handheld pies or 30–40 minutes for larger pies until golden brown on top.

Steak and Guinness Pie SERVES 4

YOU WILL NEED
25cm x 19cm pie dish

FOR THE FILLING
450g diced chuck steak
olive oil, for frying
1 onion, peeled and diced
1 leek, trimmed and sliced
1 carrot, peeled and roughly chopped
1 garlic clove, peeled and sliced
a handful of fresh thyme leaves
   (or 1 tbsp dried thyme)
a handful of fresh sage leaves
   (or 1 tbsp dried sage)
1 bay leaf
2 tbsp Worcestershire sauce,
   plus extra to taste
1 beef stock cube
1 x 500ml bottle of Original Guinness
salt and lots of freshly ground
   black pepper

FOR THE SHORTCRUST PASTRY
300g flour
a pinch of salt
150g butter
30g grated Parmesan cheese
75ml cold water
1 egg, whisked with 1 tsp cold water,
   for egg-washing and glazing

This was the very first pie I ever made. I read a few different recipes and came up with my own take on a classic. As a trial for my first pie cookery class I remember rounding up some friends, Jorja, Rose, Jacey and Michael, for a dummy run. The poor things had to endure my nervous ramblings but were very supportive with tips at the end of class. When it came to the real class I screamed when the doorbell rang, 'OMG, I have to pull this off!' I still get butterflies before classes, and say 'Showtime' in a comedy voice every time people start to arrive. (Now you know.)

First make the filling. Set a large saucepan over a high heat and brown the beef on all sides in olive oil with lots of pepper (no salt). Set aside to rest. (Too much salt at this stage will dry out your beef, when you want to keep the moisture locked in for a tender, melt-in-the-mouth texture.)

With the pan still on the heat, add some more olive oil to the pan and fry the onion, leek and carrot until soft and shiny. Return the meat and juices to the pan, throw in the garlic, herbs and Worcestershire sauce, crumble in the stock cube, season and fry for about 3 minutes.

Recipe continues overleaf

Steak and Guinness Pie CONTINUED

Pour the Guinness into the pan and mix together. Reduce the temperature to its lowest setting and cook, uncovered, for about 1½ hours, stirring occasionally, until the meat is tender and the sauce has thickened. When the sauce has finished cooking, add a dash more Worcestershire sauce for extra bite. Leave to cool.

TIP

If you want to thicken the sauce further, keep the lid off, crank up the heat and allow the liquid to cook off until you have the desired thickness.

Make the shortcrust pastry using the method on pages 17–19.

Once your pastry has chilled for 30 minutes, preheat the oven to 200°C/180°C fan/gas 6 and place a baking tray inside to heat up.

Assemble your pie using the guidelines on pages 22–25, ensuring both your pastry and filling are cold before assembly. A nice touch is to sprinkle the top of the pie with coarse sea salt and freshly ground black pepper after you've egg-washed it.

Place your pie on the hot tray in the oven and bake for 30 minutes until golden brown.

Serve with buttery new potatoes and green beans – oh yeah, and a pint of Guinness.

Favourite Festive Pies

MAKES 8–9 HANDHELD PIES OR 2 LARGE PIES

YOU WILL NEED

2 x 6-hole non-stick deep muffin trays or 2 x 20cm-round pie dishes

FOR THE WHITE SAUCE

30g butter
30g flour
400ml milk
2 tsp mustard
½ chicken stock cube
salt and freshly ground black pepper

FOR THE FILLING

3–4 pork sausages
80g lardons or smoked streaky bacon, diced
vegetable oil, for frying
1 leek, trimmed and finely sliced
2 garlic cloves, peeled and sliced
100g mushrooms, sliced
1 tbsp dried sage or a handful of chopped fresh sage leaves
100g cranberries (fresh or frozen)
50g chestnuts (vacuum-packed or canned), chopped
450g leftover turkey slices
salt and freshly ground black pepper

FOR THE SHORTCRUST PASTRY

500g plain flour
a pinch of salt
250g butter (or 125g butter and 125g lard)
125ml cold water
1 egg, whisked with 1 tsp cold water, for egg-washing and glazing

Everyone needs a simple pie recipe for leftover Christmas turkey. Gather those Christmas flavours together and bundle them into this Boxing Day feast of a pie. With turkey, sausage, chestnuts and cranberries it has lots of different textures and flavours to enjoy.

Dig out your Christmas biscuit cutters and decorate the pie lid as much as you like. I made this pie last year and tied it in a big red bow. Yes, it was a bit over the top, but it looked great and made my guests very happy.

First make the sauce. Melt the butter in a saucepan over a low heat. Once melted, whisk in the flour until you have a smooth paste (known as a roux). Add the milk, all at once, and whisk continuously for a few minutes. When the sauce starts to thicken, take the saucepan off the heat, add the mustard, crumble in the stock cube and season with salt and pepper. Continue to whisk until all the ingredients are well combined, then set aside to cool completely.

Now make the filling. Fry the sausages and lardons in a little oil over a medium heat until cooked, then spoon them out of the pan and set them aside to cool. In the same frying pan, with all the lovely sausage and bacon flavours, fry the leek for a few minutes until translucent and slightly brown. Next add the garlic and mushrooms. Continue frying for 3 minutes, then turn off the heat. Slice the sausages into bite-sized pieces.

Tip the contents of the frying pan, with all the juices, into a large mixing bowl. Add the sage, cranberries, chestnuts, turkey, sliced sausages and lardons and sauce. Mix to combine and season, to taste. Leave to cool completely.

Make the shortcrust pastry using one of the methods on pages 17–19.

Once your pastry has chilled for 30 minutes, preheat the oven to 200°C/180°C fan/gas 6 and place 2 baking trays inside to heat up.

Assemble your pies using the guidelines on pages 22–25, ensuring both your pastry and filling are cold before assembly. Use Christmas cutters to cut out shapes from the pastry scraps and stick them on with egg wash to make it look really festive.

Place your pies on the hot trays in the oven and bake for 25–30 minutes for individual pies or 30–40 minutes for large pies, until they are golden brown on top.

This pie is equally delicious hot or cold with a few pickled onions and gherkins.

Roast Chestnuts

SERVES 8

YOU WILL NEED
1kg chestnuts

I couldn't resist it: here's how to roast chestnuts for a moreish Christmas snack!

Preheat the oven to 200°C /180°C fan/ gas 6.

Using a small, sharp knife, cut a cross into the skin of each nut. Place in a roasting tin and bake for 25–30 minutes, until the skins open and the insides are tender.

To eat, peel away the tough outer skin and the pithy white inner skin to get to the sweet kernel.

Shredded Roast Chicken and Gravy Pie

MAKES ROAST DINNER FOR 2, PLUS A PIE FOR 4–8

YOU WILL NEED
25cm-round pie dish

FOR THE ROAST DINNER AND PIE FILLING
olive oil
1 x 2kg chicken
½ lemon
2 garlic cloves, peeled and bashed
8 potatoes, peeled
3 large carrots, peeled
  and roughly chopped
1 large leek, trimmed and sliced
2 sticks of celery, chopped
1 bay leaf
2 tbsp cornflour
1 chicken stock cube
a good handful of frozen peas
  (for the pie)
salt and freshly ground black pepper

FOR THE FLAKY PASTRY
120ml ice-cold water
1 tsp lemon juice
300g plain flour
a pinch of salt
100g butter
100g lard
1 egg, whisked with 1 tsp cold water,
  for egg-washing and glazing

This pie was inspired by a road trip through the Karoo in South Africa with our friends Dan, Annelie and their baby, Emily. We stopped at a little out-of-place 1950s diner and I ordered the chicken pie. They love pies in South Africa and Australia, eating them even in the hottest of temperatures. This particular pie filling was rammed with shredded roast chicken and the works, so this is how I make mine.

This is actually a recipe for two meals. When I make this pie, I first make a roast chicken dinner for two, purposely making extra trimmings and gravy and saving half of the chicken for a pie the next day. The trick to making roast chicken taste like chicken is not to add much else to it. I use a tip from my mother-in-law, Annette, to ensure maximum juiciness in the breasts: cook the chicken upside down, so that all the juices seep down into the white flesh as it cooks.

DAY 1: ROAST CHICKEN DINNER

First roast your chicken. Preheat the oven to 200°C/180°C fan/gas 6. Rub a little oil over the chicken breasts and lay breast side down in a flameproof roasting dish. Pop the lemon and crushed garlic cloves inside the bird. The only thing you do now is rub some salt and pepper into the skin: nothing else. The chicken will cook from the inside out and leave a crispy shell and juicy chicken breast. If you are tempted to turn the chicken, do it in the last 15 minutes. Adding more salt at this stage will give the bird a little more colour. Rest the chicken before carving.

As a rule, chickens should be roasted for 20 minutes per 500g, plus an extra 20 minutes, so your chicken will take around 1 hour and 40 minutes to cook.

While your chicken is roasting, prepare the vegetables. Bring a large saucepan of water to the boil. Add the potatoes and parboil for 8–10 minutes, then ladle them out and set aside. To the same saucepan add the carrots, leek and celery, a good pinch of salt and the bay leaf. Cook for a further 10 minutes. Ladle out all the veggies and set aside, covered. Keep the vegetable water for the gravy.

When your chicken has 40 minutes left to cook, remove it from the oven, add the potatoes to the roasting dish and roll them around in the chicken juices. Return the dish to the oven to finish cooking. When the chicken and potatoes are ready, transfer them to a serving dish to rest. Leave all the juices and oils in the roasting dish.

Now make the gravy. Rest the roasting dish with the juices on the hob over a low heat. Spoon in the cornflour, crumble in the stock cube and mix with a wooden spoon until it forms a paste. Now add your veggie water, a ladle at a time, stirring rapidly. The flour will drink up the water so add more and more vegetable water until you have a lovely velvety gravy that's not too runny. Season, to taste, and strain through a sieve to collect all the unwanted bits from your gravy. Make enough for around 6 people so that you have enough leftover for the pie.

Serve your roast chicken with the vegetables on the side and plenty of rich gravy over the top.

DAY 2: PIE-MAKING DAY

First prepare your filling. Gather all the leftovers. Shred the chicken (not too thinly), add the rest of the veggies, throw in the frozen peas and mix in the leftover gravy. Put everything back in the fridge to chill.

Make the flaky pastry using the method on page 20.

Once you've returned the pastry to the fridge for the second time, preheat the oven to 220°C/200°C fan/gas 7 and place a baking tray inside to heat up.

Assemble your pie using the guidelines on pages 22–25, ensuring both your pastry and filling are cold before assembly.

Place your pie on the hot tray in the oven and bake for 15 minutes, then reduce the oven temperature to 200°C /180°C fan/gas 6 and bake for a further 25–30 minutes until golden brown on top.

Serve with steamed baby carrots glazed with honey, a mixed salad and a glass of white wine.

French Onion Soup Pie (for Lovers)

SERVES 2 (MAKES 1 HUGE SOUP PIE, TO SHARE)

YOU WILL NEED

1 x 16.5cm-wide x 9cm-deep
  pudding bowl

FOR THE FILLING

1 tbsp butter
a glug of olive oil
500g onions, peeled and finely sliced
½ tsp salt
½ tsp ground black pepper
¼ tsp sugar
1½ tbsp plain flour
450ml boiling beef stock
  (made from 1 stock cube)
1 tsp wine vinegar
1 tbsp Cognac

FOR THE PUFF PASTRY

150g home-made rough puff pastry
  (see page 19) or shop-bought
  easy-roll puff pastry
30g Swiss or Gruyère cheese slice
1 egg, whisked with 1 tsp cold water,
  for egg-washing and glazing

This pie is filthy. It is so rich and intense that it must be shared. It's made to dive into and get messy. There is a Gruyère surprise in the puff pastry lid and it's a killer when the pastry falls into the soup and the cheese oozes out. Ooh là là!

First make the filling. Heat the butter and oil in a heavy-bottomed pot over a medium heat. Add the onions and fry them for 15 minutes with the lid on. Add the salt, pepper and sugar and fry for a further 20 minutes, stirring occasionally, until the onions are a dark golden colour.

Add the flour, mixing it into the onions to ensure there are no lumps. Pour in the stock and vinegar, place the lid half over the pot and simmer for a further 15 minutes.

Preheat the oven to 220°C/200°C fan/gas 7.

Recipe continues overleaf

French Onion Soup Pie
(for Lovers) CONTINUED

While you wait for your onions to simmer, get on with rolling the pastry. This is a rare recipe where you don't have to wait until all the ingredients are cold before you assemble your pie.

Cut your block of pastry in half and roll out 2 sheets of pastry to roughly the thickness of a pound coin (about 2mm). Layer the 2 sheets on top of one other. Turn the pudding bowl upside down on to the pastry and cut around the rim with a sharp knife. Remove the bowl and scraps and set aside one of the pastry circles.

Place a cheese slice in the centre of the other pastry circle and egg-wash the pastry around the cheese. Lay the other pastry circle over the top, so that the cheese is sandwiched between two circles of pastry. Prick a few holes in your cheesy pastry packet, and egg-wash the top. This is your pie lid.

Bake your pie lid on a floured tray in the oven for 10 minutes. Remove when puffed up and golden.

When your onion soup is ready, remove it from the heat and stir in the Cognac. Ladle the soup into a warm bowl and pop the pastry lid on top like a giant cheesy croûton.

Hand out big spoons and devour immediately.

Simple Veggie Pie with Blue Cheese SERVES 4

YOU WILL NEED
25cm x 19cm pie dish

FOR THE FILLING
2 tbsp butter
1 onion, peeled and finely sliced
2 sticks of celery, chopped
½ red pepper, de-seeded and
    roughly chopped
1 tbsp dried herbs, such as thyme,
    oregano or mixed herbs
1 garlic clove, peeled and chopped
1 tbsp plain flour
½ vegetable stock cube
150ml hot water or milk (if you prefer
    a creamy sauce)
100g broccoli or cauliflower florets
3 spring onions, trimmed and
    coarsely chopped
1 heaped tsp English mustard
zest of ½ lemon
60g blue cheese
salt and freshly ground pepper

FOR THE SHORTCRUST PASTRY
300g plain flour
a pinch of salt
150g butter
75ml cold water
1 tsp cumin seeds, lightly toasted
    for 2 minutes in a dry non-stick
    frying pan
1 egg, whisked with 1 tsp cold water,
    for glazing

This pie isn't too extravagant; it's easy to whip up and really tasty. It has a little kick from the lemon zest and mustard and a surprisingly deep creaminess from the blue cheese. The shortcrust pastry provides a framework that holds the sauce well.

First make the filling. Melt the butter in a large, non-stick saucepan over a medium heat. Sauté the onion, celery, red pepper and herbs for about 8 minutes, until the vegetables are tender. Add the garlic and flour and mix thoroughly. Crumble in the stock cube, add the water or milk and stir well. Throw in the broccoli or cauliflower, spring onions, mustard and lemon zest and stir to combine. Bring to the boil, then lower the heat and simmer, uncovered, for 10 minutes. Remove the pan from the heat and leave to cool slightly. Add a pinch of salt and a good grind of pepper. Mix in the cheese, then set aside to cool completely.

Make the shortcrust pastry using one of the methods on pages 17–19. The toasted cumin seeds should be added with the flour.

Once your pastry has chilled for 30 minutes, preheat the oven to 200°C/180°C fan/gas 6 and place a baking tray inside to heat up.

Assemble your pie using the guidelines on pages 22–25, ensuring both your pastry and filling are cold before assembly.

Place your pie on the hot tray in the oven and bake for 30–35 minutes until golden brown on top. Serve with steamed buttery and lemony green beans and a mixed salad.

Beef and Caramelised Onion Pie (A good pie for Father's Day)

SERVES 4

YOU WILL NEED
25cm x 19cm pie dish

FOR THE FILLING
450g stewing steak or chuck steak, diced
olive oil, for frying
1 tsp ground black pepper
25g butter
4 onions, peeled and sliced
½ tsp sugar
1 tbsp cornflour
3 sprigs of fresh rosemary
½ tsp salt
500ml boiling beef stock (made from 1½ stock cubes)

FOR THE SHORTCRUST PASTRY
300g flour
a pinch of salt
150g butter
75ml cold water
1 egg, whisked with 1 tsp cold water, for egg-washing and glazing

Flicking through my 1924 edition of *The Radiation New World Cookery Book* (a cookbook for the first home gas cookers) I was struck by the 'no frills' ingredients. For example, a beef stew recipe simply contained beef, salt, pepper and water. Inspired, I made a filling with very few ingredients but, hopefully, a lot more flavour than the original. The caramelized onions give the beef a sweetness you won't believe.

First make the filling. Set a saucepan over a high heat and brown the beef on all sides in olive oil with the black pepper (no salt). (Too much salt at this stage will dry out your beef.) Remove from the pan and set aside.

With the pan still on the heat, add the butter and a dash more olive oil (to stop the butter burning) to the pan and fry the sliced onions for a few minutes over a medium heat. Place the lid on the pan and continue to cook for 15 minutes.

Take the lid off the pan, increase the heat to high and add the sugar. Cook for another 10 minutes with the lid off until your onions are lovely and brown. Mix in the cornflour and add the rested beef and juices, the rosemary and the salt, over the hot stock, lower the heat and cook with the lid on for about 1 hour.

Okay, last 10 minutes: take the lid off, crank up the heat so that the filling can bubble away and the gravy reduces and thickens. Set aside to cool completely.

Make the shortcrust pastry using one of the methods on pages 17–19.

Once your pastry has chilled for 30 minutes, preheat the oven to 200°C/180°C fan/gas 6 and place a baking tray inside to heat up.

Assemble your pie using the guidelines on pages 22–25, ensuring both your pastry and filling are cold before assembly.

Place your pie on the hot tray in the oven and bake for 30 minutes until golden brown. Garnish with a few sprigs of rosemary and serve with buttery potato and parsnip mash.

Swe
REC

My Twin Peaks Cherry Pie

SERVES 6–8

YOU WILL NEED
22cm-round pie dish

FOR THE FILLING
110g sugar
3 level tbsp cornflour
850g cherries, de-stoned
(roughly 700g when de-stoned)
1 tbsp lemon juice
3 tbsp water
½ tsp almond essence or 1 tbsp
Amaretto

FOR THE FLAKY PASTRY
100ml ice-cold water
1 tsp lemon juice
100g butter
100g vegetable shortening
(e.g. Crisco, Trex, Cookeen)
300g plain flour
a pinch of salt
1 egg, whisked with 1 tsp cold water,
for glazing
sugar, for dusting

This is my homage to the legendary cherry pie served at the local diner in the cult series from the 1990s. *Twin Peaks* was dark, twisted and often funny. The main character, Agent Dale Cooper, was a connoisseur of cherry pie and had a famous fondness for this one. If you aren't familiar with *Twin Peaks*, it's enough to know that a fresh cherry pie is the perfect summer pie.

First make the pie filling. Mix the sugar and cornflour in a bowl then carefully drop in the cherries. Mix to coat them in the sugar, then set aside for 5 minutes.

Transfer the coated cherries to a saucepan set over a low heat and add the lemon juice, water and almond essence. Mix to combine and cook with the lid on for 7 minutes. Your aim is to break down the cherries a little to make the start of a thick juice. Watch the time carefully, and stir occasionally; you don't want the cornflour and sugar to stick to the bottom of the pan. After 7 minutes take the pan off the heat and leave to cool completely.

Make the flaky pastry using the method on page 20.

Once you've returned the pastry to the fridge for the second time, preheat the oven to 200°C/180°C fan/gas 6 and place a baking tray inside to heat up.

Assemble your pie using the guidelines on pages 22–25, ensuring both your pastry and filling are cold before assembly. Decorate it using the lattice method on page 24. Brush the white of an egg around the sides and bottom of the pastry shell and sprinkle lightly with flour before you add the filling to help the juices to stay put and give the pie a golden bottom.

Place your pie on the hot tray in the oven and bake for 15 minutes, then reduce the heat to 180°C/160°C fan/gas 4 and bake for a further 35–40 minutes until golden brown on top and the filling is bubbling up. If the pie is browning too quickly, place some foil around the crust edge, leaving the middle to bake and bubble through. Leave to cool completely.

My Twin Peaks Cherry Pie.

Little Blueberry and Lemon Tartlets
MAKES 12 MINI TARTLETS

YOU WILL NEED
12-hole patty tin

FOR THE VERSATILE TARTLET PASTRY
180g plain flour
100g butter
1½ tbsp icing sugar
1 egg white
optional: juice of ½ lemon mixed
*   with 3 tbsp icing sugar, to drizzle*

FOR THE FILLING
2 tsp cornflour
2 tbsp sugar
2 tbsp freshly squeezed lemon juice
2 tsp grated lemon zest
120g fresh blueberries

These are 'rustic' little tarts and another fast tasty morsel to serve at a shindig! The lemon zest adds freshness to the simple blueberries. The blueberry is a tough little fruit so it works well in this pie; it wouldn't work so well with softer fruit, such as strawberries and raspberries, as they have too much juice. So blueberries rule for this treat.

First make the versatile tartlet pastry and line your patty tin using the method on page 20.

Preheat the oven to 180°C/160°C fan/gas 4.

Next prepare the filling. In a small bowl mix together the cornflour, sugar, lemon juice and zest until it forms a paste. Tip the blueberries into the mixture and coat them completely. Set aside for 5 minutes, then mix again and spoon the mixture into the chilled pastry shells. Bake for about 16–18 minutes, then transfer to a wire rack to cool.

If you like, drizzle the icing sugar mixture over the tartlets before leaving them to cool.

Fresh Berry Pie SERVES 8

YOU WILL NEED
25cm-round pie dish

FOR THE SWEET SHORTCRUST PASTRY
400g plain flour, plus extra
   for sprinkling
100g butter
100g vegetable shortening
   (e.g. Crisco, Trex, Cookeen)
3 tbsp sugar, plus extra for sprinkling
100ml cold water
1 egg, whisked with 1 tsp cold water,
   for egg-washing

FOR THE FILLING
300g strawberries
100g blueberries
300g raspberries and/or blackberries
100g sugar
3 level tbsp cornflour
1 egg white

What better way to use up lovely summer berries than in a pie. This recipe reminds me of my brothers and I picking blackberries from our local Llanedeyrn woods in Cardiff and bringing them back home for mum to do something with. She would usually greet us with a huff to imply, 'I have to make a pie now, do I kids?' Just spooning in those lovely deep colours wrapped in sugary pastry with loads of cream brings a tear to my eye.

Make the sweet shortcrust pastry using one of the methods on pages 17–19.

Once the pastry has chilled for at least 30 minutes, preheat the oven to 200°C/180°C fan/gas 6 and place a baking tray inside to heat up. Grease your pie dish.

Now make the filling. Trim and rinse the fruit, then leave to dry on some kitchen roll for a few minutes. In a large bowl mix together the sugar and cornflour, then tip in all the fruit. Gently coat the fruit with the sugary mixture and leave for about 10 minutes.

Assemble your pie using the guidelines on pages 22–25, ensuring both your pastry and filling are cold before assembly. Brush egg white around the sides and bottom of the pastry shell and sprinkle lightly with flour before adding the filling.

Bake on the hot tray in the oven for 35–40 minutes until the pie is golden and the filling is bubbling out. Serve with lashings of cream.

Nectarine and Apricot Jam Tart SERVES 8

YOU WILL NEED
25cm-round non-stick loose-based
tart tin

FOR THE PASTRY
90g butter, at room temperature
40g sugar, plus extra for sprinkling
4 drops of vanilla extract
3 egg yolks
180g plain flour

FOR THE FILLING
1 tbsp flour
3 firm nectarines
3 tbsp apricot or raspberry jam
the juice of 1 lemon

When we visit friends in the summer months, I generally make this scrummy and simple tart. The pastry is a French, cakelike base, topped simply with sliced nectarines (peaches are too juicy) and drizzled with jam and lemon juice. I love moulding the pastry to the tin and the result is an ultra-thin and moreish slice of summer. Your friends will love you more if you bring this tart for dinner next time you visit.

First make the pastry. Cream together the butter and sugar with a wooden spoon. Add the vanilla and egg yolks and beat into a creamy smooth mixture. Sieve in the flour and, with your hand, combine to make a dough. Wrap it in cling film and pop it into the fridge to chill for 30 minutes.

Meanwhile, make the filling. Tip the flour into a shallow dish and set aside. With a knife, carefully cut around the centre of the nectarines and tear them apart with your hands. Remove the stones and finely slice the fruit into little half-moons.

Rest them in a colander and let the juices drain. Now sprinkle flour over the fruit (while baking the flour will absorb the excess juices to make a sauce).

Now, in a small saucepan, bring the jam and lemon juice to the boil over a medium heat. Turn off the heat and leave it to cool.

Once your pastry has chilled, preheat the oven to 170°C/150°C fan/gas 3 and place a baking tray inside to heat up. Grease your tart tin.

Roll out the chilled dough on a lightly floured surface and mould your pastry to fit the tin perfectly. Layer your fruit on top of the pastry, and drizzle the jam and lemon mixture on top. Finish off with a little sprinkling of sugar.

Bake on the hot tray in the oven for 30–35 minutes, then turn out on to a wire rack for 30 minutes to cool. Serve at room temperature with vanilla ice cream.

Apple Huckleberry 'Three Generations' Pie SERVES 8

YOU WILL NEED
25cm-round pie dish

FOR THE CRUST
450g plain flour
75g vegetable shortening
 (e.g. Crisco, Trex, Cookeen)
75g butter
1 tsp salt
1 tbsp apple cider vinegar
1 large egg
5–6 tbsp ice-cold water
1 egg, whisked with 1 tsp cold water,
 for glazing
3 tbsp sugar, for sprinkling

FOR THE FILLING
7 medium-sized organic Granny
 Smith apples, peeled and finely
 sliced
60g frozen huckleberries or blueberries
4 level tbsp cornflour
150g light brown sugar
1 heaped tsp ground cinnamon
2 tbsp butter

I wanted to include a true American apple pie recipe in this book so I contacted avid pie-maker Jessica Appelgren in San Francisco, because she knows her pie stuff. This is her family recipe. The pastry is so good that I'm tempted to only ever use this 'crust' recipe in future!

Jessica explains: 'My Grandma Hope has been making apple pie for many of her ninety years. My crust includes Grandma's two "secret ingredients": apple cider vinegar mixed with an egg for flavour and firmness in the crust. My own mom has always made the best apple pie around. Her classic filling is spot on with just the right thickness and traditional cinnamon and tart apple flavours. My addition, and what makes the pie unique, is frozen huckleberries from my dad's ranch in Oregon (but other frozen berries will also work). I love the slight tang the berries offer and huckleberries' deep purple color makes the whole pie rosy pink.'

Recipe continues overleaf

Apple Huckleberry 'Three Generations' Pie CONTINUED

Make the dough using the flaky pastry method on page 20. The only addition is to whisk the vinegar with the egg and add it to the flour mixture just before you add the water. Prepare the pie shell using the guidelines on pages 22–25 and leave it to chill in the fridge for 30 minutes.

Once your pastry has chilled, preheat the oven to 200°C/180°C fan/gas 6 and place a baking tray inside to heat up.

TIP

Huckleberries are only grown in northwest United States and Canada, and not commercially farmed. They look and taste similar to blueberries.

Now get on with the filling. Mix together all the filling ingredients, apart from the butter, and tip it into the prepared crust. Dot the butter all over the filling. Weave pastry strips in a lattice effect across the top using the method on page 24 and add a decorative border by cutting out leaf shapes from your pastry.

Bake in the oven on the hot tray for 15 minutes, then reduce the heat to 180°C/160°C fan/gas 4 and bake for a further 50–60 minutes, until the filling is thick and bubbling up. Check the pie after about 45 minutes and if the pastry is browning too quickly, place some foil around the crust edge leaving the middle to bake and bubble through.

Pretend Halloween Pumpkin Pie

SERVES 6–8

YOU WILL NEED
22cm-round loose-based flan tin

FOR THE FILLING
300g peeled sweet potato, diced
vegetable oil, for roasting
a pinch of salt
80g brown sugar
1 tbsp plain flour
1 tsp ground cinnamon
1 tsp ground ginger
½ tsp ground nutmeg
zest of ½ lemon or ½ orange
250ml evaporated milk
1 egg
1 tsp vanilla extract

FOR THE SWEET SHORTCRUST PASTRY
200g plain flour, plus extra for dusting
100g butter
2 tbsp sugar
50ml cold water
egg white
1 egg, whisked with 1 tsp cold water, for egg-washing and glazing

Pumpkins, in my opinion, are rather tasteless. So when I was asked to make some pies for a friend's Halloween party last year, I cheated and, instead of using pumpkins, used sweet potato. What a difference! The texture and the taste were much fuller and everyone said it was the best pumpkin pie they had ever tasted. Ha! Fooled you all. Of course you can use pumpkins, but I doubt I will again.

Preheat the oven to 200°C/180°C fan/gas 6 and place a baking tray inside to heat up.

Lay the diced sweet potato on a roasting tray, drizzle with a little vegetable oil, a pinch of salt and the sugar and mix to coat. Roast for 15–20 minutes, then transfer to a bowl and mash together with the dry filling ingredients. Add the evaporated milk, egg and vanilla extract, and beat together until there are no lumps.

Make the sweet shortcrust pastry using one of the methods on pages 17–19.

When the pastry has chilled, roll it out on a lightly floured surface and use it line your tin to fit perfectly. Brush around the sides and bottom of the pastry shell with the egg white and sprinkle lightly with flour. Place the tart dish on the hot baking tray (so that you don't spill the mixture) and pour the ingredients into the pastry shell. This pie doesn't have a lid, but you could use Halloween cutters in different shapes to decorate your pie. Cut out lots of shapes from scraps of pastry, then egg-wash the pie edge and fix the shapes to it. Lightly brush the surface with egg wash.

Bake on the hot tray in the oven for about 35–40 minutes until the middle is firm. Cover the pastry edges with foil if you notice they are browning too much before the middle is firm and springy.

I think this pie is even more delicious eaten cold with whipped cream.

Honey and Walnut 'Three-bites' Pies
MAKES 18 MINI PIES

YOU WILL NEED
2 x 12-hole non-stick patty tins
8.5cm-round pastry or biscuit cutter
5cm-round pastry or biscuit cutter

FOR THE CHUNKY PASTRY
50g rolled oats
170g plain flour, plus extra to dust
100g wholemeal flour
160g butter, cubed
2 tbsp sugar
1 egg, whisked with 2 tsp water
1 egg, whisked with 1 tsp cold water,
  for glazing

FOR THE FILLING
250g runny honey
zest of ½ a lemon
ground cinnamon
18 walnut halves

The first recorded recipe for pie was from Ancient Egypt, around 9500 BC. The pastry was made with wheat, oats, barley and rye, filled with honey and cooked over hot coals. Next, the Greeks borrowed the recipe and popped in nuts and fruit, bringing me to my little honey pie recipe. This pastry is chunky and wholesome enough to stand up to the rich honey filling. Devour warm or cold in three bites.

First make the pastry. Tip the oats and flours into a large bowl and mix well. Add the cubed butter and rub it into the dry ingredients, until the mixture resembles coarse breadcrumbs. This pastry will be heavier than other pastry because of the oats.

Now add the sugar, mix well, then add the whisked egg and bind together until a dough forms. Wrap the pastry in cling film and cool it in the fridge for 30 minutes.

Once your pastry has chilled, preheat the oven to 180°C/160°C fan/gas 4.

Roll out the chilled pastry on a floured surface to the thickness of a pound coin (about 2mm). Take the larger cutter and cut out 18 circles. Line your patty tins with them, leaving a slight pastry overhang for each pie.

Drizzle honey into each pastry shell (but don't over-fill them or your pies may burn). Sprinkle lemon zest and a pinch of cinnamon into each shell and place 1 walnut half in each one, to give your pies a little surprise crunch.

Roll out the remainder of the pastry until it is wafer thin, and use the smaller cutter to cut out your lids. Egg-wash the edges, top your mini pies and pinch to seal. Make a little hole in each pie lid to let the steam escape as it cooks. Egg-wash the tops.

Bake for 15 minutes (no more as they can easily burst and burn). Cool on a wire rack. Wonderful.

My Greek Baklava

MAKES 32 SMALL OR 16 LARGE PIECES

YOU WILL NEED
32cm x 21.5cm x 4cm baking tray

FOR THE SYRUP
250g granulated sugar
150g honey
200ml water
the juice of 1 lemon
1 tsp vanilla extract

FOR THE FILLING
250g walnuts
125g caster sugar
1 tbsp ground cinnamon

FOR THE PASTRY
250g butter, clarified
*   (see method, right)*
500g shop-bought filo pastry
24 cloves

I am very proud of this recipe. I had many test runs before I got it as authentic as possible. Some might argue that this isn't a pie but, in its defence, it does have a filo pastry top and bottom. Greek baklava is different to Turkish baklava: lemon, cinnamon and vanilla heighten the taste and, in my opinion, set it apart. Please try it; it's easier than you think to make (now the work is done for you!) and you will be very impressed with yourself. These are great eaten with a coffee in the morning or served with a little dollop of vanilla ice cream for dessert or an afternoon treat.

First make the syrup. Heat the sugar, honey and water in a small saucepan over a high heat until it starts to bubble. Add the lemon juice and vanilla, then lower the heat and simmer for 15–20 minutes. Don't let the syrup get too thick, and remove it if it looks like it might be. Set aside to cool.

Next prepare the filling. Tip the walnuts, sugar and cinnamon into a mixer and pulse for a few seconds (or crush them in a plastic bag using the end of a rolling pin or a pestle). Set aside.

Preheat the oven to 170°C/150°C fan/gas 3.

Now, clarify the butter for the pastry. Heat the butter in a small saucepan over a medium heat. When the butter is melted, turn off the heat. You will find that the creamy milk solids have floated to the top; spoon these out and discard. This will leave you with a golden clarified butter.

Recipe continues overleaf

My Greek Baklava CONTINUED

Lay out the filo and place your baking tray on top. Using your tray as a template, cut around the bottom edge with a sharp knife. Butter the base of the tray and quickly (or the filo will dry out) place 1 sheet of filo pastry in the bottom, brush it all over with butter and repeat until you have 10 layered, buttered sheets.

Spread half of the filling mixture evenly over the pastry layers, then repeat with another 10 sheets of filo, buttering between each one as you go. Spread the rest of the filling on top and press down a little. Repeat the filo and buttering process until you have used up all the pastry (probably another 12 sheets; use the off-cuts, as well). Butter the top, then take a sharp knife and score little squares or diamonds, cutting right down to the base of the dish. Crown each piece with a clove.

Bake your baklava for 20 minutes, then increase the heat to 200°C/180°C fan/gas 6 and bake for a further 10 minutes until golden brown.

Take the baklava out of the oven and immediately pour the syrup over the top; it will bubble and sizzle. Leave to cool.

TIP

Never keep your baklava in the fridge; store it in an airtight container

Easy Christmas Mince Pies with Chocolate Pastry MAKES 12

YOU WILL NEED
12-hole non-stick patty tray
5.5cm-round fluted pastry cutter
a small star pastry or biscuit cutter

FOR THE MINCEMEAT
Makes twice as much filling as you need,
but store in the fridge for up to a week
ready for another Christmas knees-up!)
50ml cranberry juice
50ml port
80g soft dark brown sugar
2 cooking apples, peeled and cored
80g currants
80g sultanas
50g flaked almonds
1 tsp ground cinnamon
1 tsp ground allspice
½ tsp ground ginger
¼ tsp ground cloves
½ tsp vanilla extract
2 tbsp treacle

FOR THE SWEET
SHORTCRUST PASTRY
200g plain flour
a pinch of salt
50g butter
25g cocoa powder
50g vegetable shortening
   (e.g. Crisco, Trex, Cookeen)
25g sugar
50ml cold water
1 egg, whisked with 1 tsp cold water,
   for glazing

It's so much more special to make your own mincemeat than to buy shop-bought. It doesn't take that long to make either; in fact you can make the filling and pastry all in one go. I love a good Christmas tradition, and mince-pie making is one of mine: every year, with a couple of friends (and a few drinks), we get down to making these.

First make the mincemeat. Put the cranberry juice, port and brown sugar into a saucepan over a low heat and stir gently until the sugar has completely dissolved. Add the rest of the mincemeat ingredients, apart from the vanilla and treacle, and continue to bubble away for about 15–20 minutes, stirring occasionally – be careful not to let the mixture stick to the pan. Remove from the heat and leave to cool slightly, then add the vanilla extract and treacle and give it a good stir. Roughly break down the mixture by mashing it with a wooden spoon. (Little pies = no large lumps.) Leave the mixture to cool completely.

Make the sweet shortcrust pastry using one of the methods on pages 17–19, adding the cocoa powder with the flour and butter.

Once your pastry has chilled for 30 minutes, preheat the oven to 180°C/160°C fan/gas 4. Grease your patty tray.

On a lightly floured surface, roll out the pastry to the thickness of a pound coin (about 2mm). Cut out 12 circles, each one larger than the size of a patty hole. Press them into the holes. Cut out 12 stars from the remaining pastry.

Drop a teaspoonful of cold mincemeat into each pastry case and top with a pastry star lid. Lightly brush the tops with egg wash.

Bake for 12–15 minutes until the pastry is crisp; they don't take long, so watch them to make sure they don't burn. Transfer to a wire rack to cool.

Chocolate, Date and Ginger Tart

SERVES 8

YOU WILL NEED

*21.5cm non-stick loose-based round
    tart tin, or impress with a
    36cm x 12cm x 3cm tart tin*

FOR THE FILLING

75ml double cream
75ml full-fat milk
1½ tbsp soft dark brown sugar
100g dark chocolate
1 tsp ground ginger
2 eggs
80g dates, stoned
the seeds from 1 pomegranate

FOR THE VERSATILE TARTLET PASTRY

210g plain flour
a pinch of salt
120g butter
1½ tbsp icing sugar
1 egg white

This tart is for all the chocolate lovers – an idea for a Valentine's dessert, perhaps? Although dark chocolate and ginger is a classic flavour combination, I've also added dates. Don't shy away from dates in your baking; they are so delicious and have a natural sweetness so you can reduce your sugar quantities, too. When you bite into a piece of date in this pie it tastes just like soft toffee. The pastry is dead easy and the buttery crispness complements the softness of the filling.

First make the filling. Slowly heat the cream, milk and sugar together in a saucepan over a low heat, stirring with a wooden spoon. When the mixture is bubbling slightly, remove it from heat, add the chocolate and ginger and stir well until the chocolate has melted.

Whisk the eggs for a few minutes, getting lots of air into them, then fold into the chocolate mixture. Leave to cool completely.

Make the versatile tartlet pastry and line your tin using the method on page 20.

Preheat the oven to 180°C/160°C fan/gas 4 and place a baking tray inside to heat up. Brush egg white around the sides and bottom of the pastry shell and sprinkle lightly with flour. Pour the chocolate mixture into your pastry shell and evenly dot the dates over the top. This pie does not have a lid.

Bake for 35–40 minutes on the tray in the oven until the chocolate filling is firm but still a little springy to the touch, and the pastry is golden. Transfer to a wire rack, then dab a pastry brush into a little cold water and brush lightly all over the top of the chocolate filling. The water keeps it moist and opens the bubbles in the filling so that air can escape faster.

Once cool, sprinkle the top with pomegranate seeds and serve with whipped cream.

Storing, reheating and COOKING from FROZEN

IN MY HOUSE THERE IS NO SUCH THING AS LEFTOVER PIE!

However, if you do have some leftovers, or you simply want to make a lot of pies, here are some tried and tested tips.

Pies containing cream, custard or eggs should be refrigerated once they have cooled to room temperature.

Fruit pies will keep at room temperature for 2 days, stored in an airtight plastic container or wrapped in cling film.

Savoury pies should only be refrigerated when they have cooled completely.

You can leave pastry in the fridge for up to 4 days. Don't roll it straight from the fridge; leave it on your kitchen worktop for 15 minutes to warm up a bit first.

You can also leave your baked pies in the fridge for up to 4 days. Cool them to room temperature first and wrap them in cling film.

To reheat your pies from the fridge, preheat the oven to 200°C/180°C fan/gas 6 and bake for 15–20 minutes. The filling needs to be thoroughly heated through before serving. If the pastry top is browning too quickly, cover the pie with foil halfway through cooking.

You can freeze pastry, wrapped in cling film, for up to 3 months. Mark the date on it so you know how old it is. Defrost completely in the fridge and then stand it on your kitchen worktop to warm up a bit before rolling.

It's a good idea to make your pies and freeze them uncooked. That way you can make a big batch and take a pie out (to bake from frozen) whenever you want.

Frozen fruit pies will keep for up to 4 months in the freezer. Frozen meat or veggie pies will keep for 3 months.

To cook unbaked pies from frozen, just add 15 minutes to the original baking time. For example, if your pie recipe said bake for 25 minutes, then your new bake time for your frozen pie will be 40 minutes – and always in a preheated oven, usually at 200°C /180°C fan/gas 6. (Oven temperatures may vary according to recipe.) Do not thaw the pie before baking.

To serve a prebaked pie from frozen, thaw it at room temperature for 1½ hours, then bake on the lowest shelf of a preheated oven, usually at 200°C/180°C fan/gas 6 for 35 minutes until hot all the way through. (Oven temperatures may vary according to recipe.)

Conversion CHARTS

WEIGHTS

METRIC	IMPERIAL
10 g	½ oz
20 g	¾ oz
25 g	1 oz
40 g	1½ oz
50 g	2 oz
60 g	2½ oz
75 g	3 oz
110 g	4 oz
125 g	4½ oz
150 g	5 oz
175 g	6 oz
200 g	7 oz
225 g	8 oz
250 g	9 oz
275 g	10 oz
350 g	12 oz
450 g	1 lb
700 g	1 lb 8 oz
900 g	2 lb
1.35 kg	3 lb

VOLUMES

METRIC	IMPERIAL
55 ml	2 fl oz
75 m	3 fl oz
150 ml	5 fl oz (¼ pint)
275 ml	10 fl oz (½ pint)
570 ml	1 pint
725 ml	1¼ pints
1 litre	1¾ pints
1.2 litres	2 pints
1.5 litres	2½ pints
2.25 litres	4 pint

OVEN TEMPERATURES

°C	GAS MARK	°F
140°C	1	275°F
150°C	2	300°F
170°C	3	325°F
180°C	4	350°F
190°C	5	375°F
200°C	6	400°F
220°C	7	425°F
230°C	8	450°F
240°C	9	475°F

Note: If you are using a fan oven you will need to reduce the oven temperature given in the recipe by 20 degrees

AMERICAN LIQUID CONVERSIONS

METRIC	IMPERIAL	AMERICAN
15 ml	½ fl oz	1 tbsp
30 ml	1 fl oz	1/8 cup
60 ml	2 fl oz	¼ cup
120 ml	4 fl oz	½ cup
240 ml	8 fl oz	1 cup
480 ml	16 fl oz	1 pint

AMERICAN CUP CONVERSIONS

METRIC	IMPERIAL	AMERICAN
150 g	5 oz	1 cup flour
225 g	8 oz	1 cup caster/granulated sugar
175 g	6 oz	1 cup brown sugar
225 g	8 oz	1 cup butter/margarine/lard
200 g	7 oz	1 cup sultanas/raisins
150 g	5 oz	1 cup currants
110 g	4 oz	1 cup ground almonds
350 g	12 oz	1 cup golden syrup
200 g	7 oz	1 cup uncooked rice
110 g	4 oz	1 cup grated cheese

ACKNOWLEDGEMENTS

There I was sitting at my laptop in a new-mum haze, overtired from colicky days and colicky nights, when an email arrived from a Jane Graham Maw (Graham Maw Christie Literary Agency) saying she likes what I do, if I ever want to write a book to give her a call.

My first thought was, 'What am I going to write a cookery book about?' My second thought was to give it some more thought! So I pretty much forgot about it, being in a baby-brain state of distraction.

My encouraging partner, Clive Kelly, egged me on to contact Jane; he was very excited and said I was stupid not to at least meet her.

I still wasn't convinced, but one morning I bolted straight up (this time not my daughter waking me) with an idea for a cookery book.

I quickly rushed to my laptop and started the layout to a fantastic new cookery concept. I was now excited and contacted Jane.

We met in Covent Garden for tea, and I prattled on about my idea. When I had finished, feeling I had made a good pitch, Jane rather calmly said, 'Keep that for your second book, I was thinking a book of pies.'

I contacted my friend Noah Crutchfield, from Maiden Gift Shop. He introduced me to Square Peg books and suggested some ideas.

I aimed my proposal largely at Square Peg; I loved their style and thought this was the publisher for me.

Jane set up a couple of publishing meetings, which were exciting, but they wanted totally different pie books – 100 pie recipes and the like. Hmm, too much work with a new baby, I thought.

Jane advised me to just go with one, when on that very same day, Square Peg, as if by magic, contacted Jane and wanted a meeting.

I remember screaming with joy after our chat over the phone.

Walking through the doors of Random House was exhilarating. I brought along a few boxes of my Twin Peaks Cherry Pies to try and impress. I instantly warmed to Rosemary Davidson and Caroline McArthur; they didn't want to change a thing! Wow. How many years have I waited for someone to say that in the music industry?!

I want to also thank the hundreds of brilliant pie apprentices over the years who have joined the fun at my Proper British Pie classes! Thank you for the support from my family, friends and the lovely press, Muswell Hill Bakery, Central Street Cookery School for letting me loose in their kitchens to run my classes, and not forgetting all the cookery assistants I've exhausted over the years.

Thanks Caroline for your wonderful style ideas and for working closely with me on the book. And thanks Martha Parava for some cool props.

Finally, thanks Phaedra for letting Mummy write her book and make pies during your afternoon naps, and to you again, Clive, for eating all those pies!

Let them eat Pie!

Index

ABOUT MARIKA

Marika Gauci is an Anglo-Greek former singer-songwriter and performer who traded a life of rock 'n' roll for a life in the glorious food industry. After assisting in prestigious cookery schools and working as a chef, she cut loose and formed her own unique home cookery school in London, Marika's Kitchen.

Word of London's only pie-making classes quickly spread, the media came calling and Marika found herself guesting as a pie expert on the Good Food Network and chatting live on BBC Radio London, while rave reviews came in from such luminaries as Delia Online, *Olive* magazine and more. Following the birth of her daughter, Marika has now returned to action, steering Marika's Kitchen to further success.

www.marikas-kitchen.com